THE HOLLOW CROWN

The Normans: William I, William II, Henry I, Stephen,
from Matthew Paris

First published in this edition in Great Britain 1971 by
Hamish Hamilton Ltd,
90 Great Russell Street, London WC1.

Designed by Jim Gibson.

Type set by Westerham Press Ltd.,
Printed in Great Britain by Jarrold and Sons Ltd., Norwich.

The follies, foibles and faces of the Kings and Queens of
England

The Hollow Crown

Devised by John Barton
Picture research by Joy Law

HAMISH HAMILTON   LONDON

The follies, foibles and faces of the Kings and Queens of England

The Hollow Crown

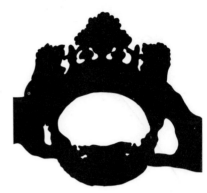

Devised by John Barton
Picture research by Joy Law

HAMISH HAMILTON   LONDON

First published in this edition in Great Britain 1971 by
Hamish Hamilton Ltd,
90 Great Russell Street, London WC1.

Designed by Jim Gibson.

Type set by Westerham Press Ltd.,
Printed in Great Britain by Jarrold and Sons Ltd., Norwich.

ILLUSTRATIONS

PROLOGUE

For God's sake, let us sit upon the ground   *Richard*
And tell sad stories of the death of kings:
How some have been depos'd; some slain in war;
Some haunted by the ghosts they have depos'd;
Some poison'd by their wives; some sleeping kill'd;
All murder'd – for within the hollow crown
That rounds the mortal temples of a king
Keeps Death his court; and there the antic sits,
Scoffing his state and grinning at his pomp;
Allowing him a breath, a little scene,
To monarchize, be fear'd, and kill with looks;
Infusing him with self and vain conceit,
As if this flesh, which walls about our life,
Were brass impregnable; and humour'd thus,
Comes at the last, and with a little pin
Bores through his castle wall, and farewell, king!

From William Shakespeare *Richard II.*

the Normans

Coin of William I

In 1930 Sellars and Yeatman wrote *1066 and All that,*
a history of England of which they said 'it contains all the
history you can remember.'

In the year 1066 occurred the other memorable date in
English History, viz. *William the Conqueror, Ten Sixty-six.*
This is also called *The Battle of Hastings,* and was when
William I (1066) conquered England at the Battle of Senlac
(*Ten Sixty-six*).
  When William the Conqueror landed he lay down on

the beach and swallowed two mouthfuls of sand. This was
his first conquering action and was in the South; later be
ravaged the North as well.

The Norman Conquest was a Good Thing, as from this
time onwards England stopped being conquered and thus
was able to become top nation.

William Rufus was always very angry and red in the face and was
therefore unpopular, so that his death was a Good Thing.

Henry I was famous for his handwriting and was therefore
generally called Henry Beau-geste. He was extremely fond
of his son William, who was, however, drowned in the
White City. Henry tried to console himself for his loss by
eating a surfeit of palfreys. This was a Bad Thing since he
died of it and *never smiled again.*

The moment Stephen came to the throne it was realized
that he was a mistake and had been christened wrong; thus
everything was thrown into confusion.

Stephen himself felt quite uncalled for, and even his Aunt
Matilda was able to take him in when she began announcing
that she was the real King. Stephen, however, soon discovered
that she had been mal-christened, too, and was unable to
say for certain whether her name was Matilda or Maud.

After this Stephen and Matilda (or Maud) spent the reign
escaping from each other over the snow in nightgowns
while 'God and His Angels slept.'

Our knowledge of the Norman kings comes from the
early chroniclers who have left us pen portraits of them
which, despite their authors' biases, tend to agree with
each other and may be accepted as reasonably accurate.
The Anglo-Saxon Chronicle says of William I :

One thousand and eighty-seven years after the nativity of our
Lord Jesus Christ, in the twenty-first year of William's rule
and reign over England, the king fell sick of the evil
and died.

Alas! how deceitful and transitory is the prosperity of
this world. He who was once a mighty king, and lord of
many a land, was left of all the land with nothing save
seven feet of ground: and he who was once decked with
gold and jewels, lay then covered over with earth.

The Abbaye aux Hommes,
Caen founded by William I

He was of just stature, ordinary corpulence, fierce countenance; his forehead was bare of hair; of such great strength of arm, that it was often a matter of surprise, that no one was able to draw his bow, which himself could bend when his horse was on full gallop; he was majestic whether sitting or standing, although the protuberance of his belly deformed his royal person; of excellent health so that he was never confined with any dangerous disorder, except at the last; so given to the pleasures of the chase, that as I have before said, ejecting the inhabitants, he let a space of many miles grow desolate that, when at liberty from other

The Abbaye aux Dames, Caen,
where Matilda of Flanders
is buried

avocations, he might there pursue his pleasures.

His anxiety for money is the only thing on which he can deservedly be blamed. This he sought all opportunities of scraping together, he cared not how; he would say and do some things and indeed almost anything, unbecoming to such great majesty, where the hope of money allured him. I have here no excuse whatever to offer, unless it be, as one has said, that 'of necessity he must fear many, whom many fear'.

From William of Malmesbury *Historia Anglorum.*

Coin of William II

William I was succeeded by his son, William Rufus.

Greatness of soul was pre-eminent in the king, which, in process of time, he obscured by excessive severity; vices, indeed, in place of virtues, so insensibly crept into his bosom, that he could not distinguish them. The world doubted, for a long time, whither he would incline; what tendency his disposition would take. At first, as long as archbishop Lanfranc survived, he abstained from every crime; so that it might be hoped, he would be the very mirror of kings. After his death, for a time, he showed himself so variable, that the balance hung even betwixt vices and virtues. At last, however, in his latter years, the desire after good grew cold, and the crop of evil increased to ripeness: his liberality became prodigality; his magnanimity pride; his austerity cruelty.

He was, when abroad, and in public assemblies, of supercilious look, darting his threatening eye on the by-stander; and with assumed severity and ferocious voice, assailing such as conversed with him. From apprehension of poverty, and of the treachery of others, as may be conjectured, he was too much given to lucre, and to cruelty. At home and at table, with his intimate companions, he gave loose to levity and to mirth. He was a most facetious railer at any thing he had himself done amiss, in order that he might thus do away with obloquy, and make it matter of jest. He was a man who knew not how to take off from the price of any thing, or to judge of the value of goods; but the trader might sell him his commodity at whatever rate, or the soldier demand any pay he pleased. He was anxious that the cost of his clothes should be extravagant, and angry if they were purchased at a low price. One morning, indeed, while putting on his new boots, he asked his chamberlain what they cost; and when he replied, 'Three shillings,' indignantly and in a rage he cried out, 'You son of a whore, how long has the king worn boots of so paltry a price? Go, and bring me a pair worth a mark of silver.' He went, and bringing him a much cheaper pair, told him, falsely, that they cost as much as he had ordered: 'Aye', said the king, 'these are suitable to royal majesty.' Thus his chamberlain used to charge him what he pleased for his clothes; acquiring by these means many things for his own advantage.

From William of Malmesbury *Historia Anglorum*.

He was very harsh and fierce in his rule over his realm, and towards his followers and to all his neighbours, and very terrifying. Influenced by the advice of evil councillors, which was always gratifying to him, and by his own covetousness, he was continually exasperating this nation with depredations and unjust taxes. In his days, therefore, righteousness declined, and evil of every kind towards God and man put up its head. Everything that was hateful to God and to righteous men was the daily practice in this land during his reign. Therefore he was hated by almost all his people and abhorrent to God. This his end testified, for he died in the midst of his sins without repentance or any atonement for his evil deeds.

On the morning after Lammas, king William was killed with an arrow while hunting by one of his men. He was afterwards brought to Winchester, and buried in the cathedral in the thirteenth year of his reign.

A few of the peasants carried his corpse to the cathedral at Winchester on a horse drawn wagon with blood dripping from it the whole way. There in the cathedral crossing, under the tower, he was interred, in the presence of many great men, mourned by few. Next year there followed the tower's collapse. I forbear to tell the opinions which were held on this event, lest I seem to believe in trifles – especially since it would have collapsed in any case, even if he had not been buried there, because it was badly built.

From the Anglo-Saxon Chronicle.

Henry I, to whom the epithet 'beauclerc' was given in
the fourteenth century, was literate, unlike his father
and grandfather but we still have to rely on the
chroniclers for our knowledge of his person.

*Manuscript portrayal of
Henry I*

He was of middle stature: his hair was black, but scanty
near the forehead; his eyes mildly bright; his chest brawny;
his body fleshy; he was facetious in proper season, nor did
multiplicity of business cause him to be less pleasant when
he mixed in society. Not prone to personal combat, he
verified the saying of Scipio Africanus, 'My mother bore me
a commander, not a soldier;' wherefore he was inferior in
wisdom to no king of modern time; and, as I may almost
say, he clearly surpassed all his predecessors in England and
preferred contending by counsel, rather than by the sword.
If he could, he conquered without bloodshed; if it was
unavoidable, with as little as possible. He was free, during
his whole life, from impure desires; for, as we have learned
from those who were well informed, he was led by female
blandishments, not for the gratification of incontinency, but
for the sake of issue; nor condescended to casual intercourse, unless where it might produce that effect; in this
respect the master of his natural inclinations, not the
passive slave of lust. He was plain in his diet, rather
satisfying the calls of hunger, than surfeiting himself by

*Matilda of Scotland depicted
in the Golden Book of St Albans*

variety of delicacies. He never drank but to allay thirst; execrating the least departure from temperance, both in himself and in those about him. He was heavy to sleep, which was interrupted by frequent snoring. His eloquence was rather unpremeditated than laboured; not rapid, but deliberate.

From William of Malmesbury *Historia Anglorum.*

On the death of the great King Henry, his character was freely canvassed by the people, as is usual after men are dead. Some contended that he was eminently distinguished for his three brilliant gifts. These were, great sagacity, for his counsels were profound, his foresight keen, and his eloquence commanding; success in war, for, besides other splendid achievements, he was victorious over the King of France; and wealth, in which he far surpassed all his predecessors. Others however taking a different view, attributed to him three gross vices; avarice, as though his wealth was great, in imitation of his progenitors he importuned the people by taxes and exactions, entangling them in the toils of his informers; cruelty, in that he plucked out the eyes of his kinsman, the Earl of Morton, in his captivity, though the horrid deed was unknown till death revealed the king's secrets; and they mentioned other instances of which I will say nothing; and wantonness for, like Solomon, he was perpetually enslaved by female seductions. Such remarks were freely bruited abroad. But in the troublesome times which succeeded from the atrocities of the Normans, whatever King Henry had done, either despotically, or in the regular exercise of his royal authority, appeared in comparison most excellent.

He devoured lampreys, which always disagreed with him, though he was excessively fond of them; and when his physicians forbad him to eat them the king did not heed their wise advice. This feast, then provoking an evil humour, (it is an active cause of such things), cooling his aged frame to a fatal degree, set up a sudden and extreme disturbance. His constitution, struggling against this, excited an acute fever by way of frustrating the attack of the hurtful matter. But since he could withstand it by no means, the great king died on the first day of December.

From Henry of Huntingdon *Historia Anglorum.*

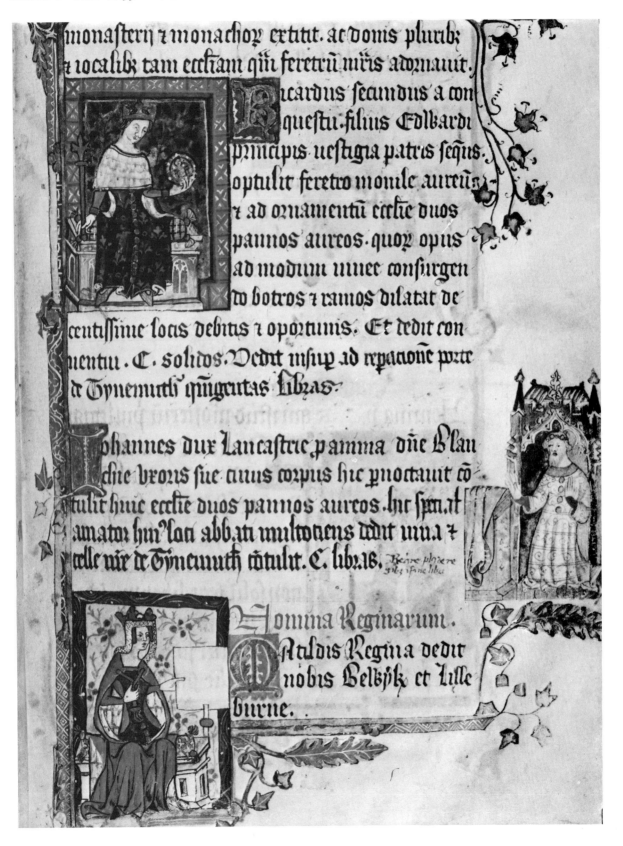

Coin of Stephen

Henry's son William had been drowned in the White Ship, and his daughter Matilda succeeded him. But her claim to the throne was disputed by her cousin Stephen and civil war broke out.

In the days of this King there was nothing but strife, evil, and robbery, for quickly the great men who were traitors rose against him. When the traitors saw that Stephen was a good-humoured, kindly, and easy-going man who inflicted no punishment, then they committed all manner of horrible crimes. They had done him homage and sworn oaths of fealty to him, but not one of their oaths was kept. They were all forsworn and their oaths broken. For every great man built him castles and held them against the King; and they filled the whole land with these castles. They sorely burdened the unhappy people of the country with forced labour on the castles; and when the castles were built, they filled them with devils and wicked men. By night and by day they seized those whom they believed to have any wealth, whether they were men or women; and in order to get their gold and silver, they put them into prison and tortured them with unspeakable tortures, for never were martyrs tortured as they were. They hung them up by the feet and smoked them with foul smoke. They strung them up by the thumbs, or by the head, and hung coats of mail on their feet. They tied knotted cords round their heads and twisted it till it entered the brain. They put them in dungeons wherein were adders and snakes and toads, and so destroyed them. Many thousands they starved to death.

I know not how to, nor am I able to tell of, all the atrocities nor all the cruelties which they wrought upon the unhappy people of this country. It lasted throughout the nineteen years that Stephen was King, and always grew worse and worse. Never did a country endure greater misery, and never did the heathen act more vilely than they did.

And so it lasted for nineteen years while Stephen was King, till the land was all undone and darkened with such deeds, and men said openly that Christ and his angels slept.

From the Anglo-Saxon Chronicle.

THE PLANTAGENETS

34

Each generation rewrites history to suit itself: in 1675 Sir Winston Churchill Kt wrote introductory notes to his history.

Henry II Plantagenet, the first of that name and race, and the very greatest King that England ever knew, but withal the most unfortunate, and that which made his misfortunes more notorious was, that they rose out of his own bowels; his death being imputed to those only to whom himself had given life, his ungracious sons, the eldest whereof that survived him, succeeded by the name of

Richard I, Cœur-de-Lion, whose undutifulness to his father was so far retorted by his brother, that looking on it as a just judgment upon him when he died he desired to be buried as near his father as might be possible, in hopes to meet the sooner, and ask forgiveness of him in the other world. His brother

John, surnamed Lackland, had so much more lack of grace, that he had no manner of sense of his offence, though alike guilty; who after all his troubling the world, and being troubled with it, neither could keep the crown with honour, nor leave it in peace, which made it a kind of miracle, that so passionate a prince as his son

Henry III should bear up so long as he did, who made a shift to shuffle away fifty-six years doing nothing, or which was worse, time enough to have overthrown the tottering monarchy, had it not been supported by such a noble pillar as was his son and successor

Edward I, a prince worthy of greater empire than he left him; who being a strict observer of opportunity (the infallible sign of wisdom) composed all the differences that had indebted his father's, grandfathers' and great-grandfathers' governments; and had questionless died as happy as he was glorious, had his son

Edward II answered expectation, who had nothing to glory
in, but that he was the son of such a father, and the father
of such a son as

Edward III who was no less fortunate than valiant, and his
fortune the greater by a kind of anti-peristasis, as coming
between two unfortunate princes, successor to his father
and predecessor to his grandson

Richard II, the most unfortunate son of that most fortunate
father Edward, commonly called the Black Prince; who
not having the judgment to distinguish between flatterers
and friends, fell (like his great-grandfather) the miserable
example of credulity, being deposed by his cousin

Henry IV, the first King of the house of Lancaster, descending
from a fourth son of Edward the third, who being so much
a greater subject than he was a king, 'twas thought he took
the crown out of compassion rather than ambition, to
relieve his oppressed country, rather than to raise his own
house; and accordingly providence was pleased to rivet him
so fast in the opinion of the people, that his race have
continued (though not without great interruption) ever
since. His son

Henry V was in that repute with the people, that they
swore allegiance to him before he was crowned; an honour
never done to any of his predecessors; neither was he less
singular in his fortune than his glory; having united the
lilies of France to the roses of England, and made of both
one diadem, to place on the head of his son

Henry VI, who whilst he was a child could have no sense of
the honour or happiness he was born to; and when he came
to be a man so despised it, that everybody thought him
fitter to be a priest than a king; only those of the house of
York thought him fitter to be made a sacrifice than a priest;
and accordingly crook-backed Richard murdered him to
make way for his elder brother

Edward IV the first King of the house of York, descended from the fifth son of Edward the third, who made the white rose to flourish as long as Henry the fourth did the red; and had kept it flourishing much longer, had he not been more unfortunate, by the ambition of those of his own, than those of his enemies' faction. His two sons

Edward V that should have succeeded him, with his innocent brother, being both murdered by their unnatural uncle (who yet called himself their protector)

Richard III, Duke of Gloucester, who having killed one king before to make way for their father, killed them afterward to make way for himself, but his usurpation lasted a very little while, both nature and providence agreeing to deny him any children of his own, for that he had so ill treated those of his nearest relation, so that for want of issue, rather than want of success, the crown came to the house of Lancaster.

Henry II, the son of William I's daughter Matilda and Geoffrey of Anjou called Plantagenet, brought strong rule back to the country.

Coin of Henry II

He was somewhat red of face, and broad-breasted; short of body, and therewithal fat, which made him use much exercise, and little meat. He was commonly called Henry Shortmantle, because he was the first that brought the use of short cloaks out of Anjou into England. Concerning endowments of mind, he was of a spirit in the highest degree generous; which made him often say, that all the world sufficed not to a courageous heart. His custom was to be always in action; for which cause, if he had no real wars, he would have feigned; and would transport forces either into Normandy or Britanny, and go with them himself, whereby he was always prepared of an army; and made it a schooling to his soldiers, and to himself an exercise. To his children he was both indulgent and hard; for out of indulgence he caused his son Henry to be crowned King in his own time; and out of hardness he caused his younger sons to rebel against him. He was rather superstitious than not religious; while he showed more by his carriage towards Becket being dead than while he lived. His inconstancy was not so much that he used other women besides his wife, but that he used the affianced wife of his own son. He married Eleanor, daughter of William Duke of Guienne, late wife of Lewis the Seventh of France. Some say King Lewis carried her into the Holy Land, where she carried herself not very holily, but led a licentious life; and, which is the worst kind of licentiousness, in carnal familiarity with a Turk.

From Sir Richard Baker *A Chronicle of the Kings of England.*

Queen Eleanor was a sick woman,
　And afraid that she should die;
Then she sent for two friars of France,
　For to speak with them speedily.

The King called down his nobles all,
　By one, by two, and by three;
'Earl Marshall, I'll go shrive the Queen,
　And thou shalt wend with me!'

'A boon, a boon!' quoth Earl Marshall,
　And fell on his bended knee,
'That whatsoe'er the Queen may say,
　No harm thereof may be.'

'I'll pawn my living and my lands,
    My sceptre and my crown,
That whatever Queen Eleanor says,
    I will not write it down.'

'Do you put on one friar's coat,
    And I'll put on another,
And we will to Queen Eleanor go,
    One friar like another.'

Thus both attired then they go;
    When they came to Whitehall,
The bells they did ring, and the choristers sing,
    And the torches did light them all.

When that they came before the Queen,
    They fell on their bended knee:
'A boon, a boon! our gracious queen,
    That you sent so hastily.'

'Are you two friars of France?' she said,
    'Which I suppose you be;
But if you are two English friars,
    Then hanged shall you be.'

'We are two friars of France,' they said,
    'As you suppose we be;
We have not been at any mass
    Since we came from the sea.'

'The first vile thing that ere I did
    I will to you unfold;
Earl Marshall had my maidenhead,
    Underneath this cloth of gold.'

'That is a vile sin,' then said the king,
    'God may forgive it thee!'
'Amen! Amen!' quoth Earl Marshall,
    With a heavy heart then spoke he.

*Tomb of Eleanor of Aquitaine
in Fontevrault Abbey*

*Tomb of Henry II in
Fontevrault Abbey*

'The next vile thing that ere I did
  To you I'll not deny;
I made a box of poison strong,
  To poison King Henry.'

'That is a vile sin,' then said the King,
  'God may forgive it thee!'
'Amen! Amen!' quoth Earl Marshall,
  'And I wish it so may be.'

'The next vile thing that ere I did
  To you I will discover;
I poisoned Fair Rosamund,
  All in fair Woodstock bower.'

'That is a vile sin,' then said the King,
  'God may forgive it thee.'
'Amen! Amen!' quoth Earl Marshall,
  'And I wish it so may be.'

'Do you see yonders little boy,
  A tossing of that ball?
That is Earl Marshall's eldest son,
  And I love him the best of all.

'Do you see yonders little boy,
  A catching of the ball?
That is King Henry's son,' she said,
  'And I love him the worst of all.

'His head is like unto a bull,
  His nose is like a boar;'
'No matter for that,' King Henry said,
  'I love him the better therefore.'

The King pull'd off his friar's coat,
  And appeared all in red;
She shriek'd and she cry'd, she wrung her hands,
  And said she was betray'd.

> The King look'd over his left shoulder,
>   And a grim look looked he,
> And said, 'Earl Marshall, but for my oath,
>   Then hanged shouldst thou be.'

A ballad called 'Queen Eleanor's Confession'.

He was out of measure given to fleshly lust; for not contented with the use of his wife, he kept many concubines. But namely he delighted most in the company of a pleasant damsel, whom he called the rose of the world (the common people named her Rosamund) for her passing beauty, being verily a rare and peerless piece in those days. He made her an house at Woodstock in Oxfordshire, like a labyrinth, that no creature might find her or come to her except he were instructed by the King. But the common report of the people is that the Queen in the end found her out by a silken thread, which the King had drawn after him out of her chamber with his foot, and dealt with her in such sharp and cruel wise, that she lived not long thereafter.

From Rafael Holinshed *Chronicles of England*.

She was buried at Godstow, in a house of nuns, with these verses upon her tomb :

> The rose of the world, but not the clean flower,
>   Is now here graven, to whom beauty was lent.
> In this grave, full dark, is now her bower,
>   That by her life was sweet and redolent.
> But now that she is from this life blent,
>   Though she were sweet, now foully doth she stink,
> A mirror, good, for all men that on her think.

From John Stow *Chronicles*.

Richard, like John and his two other brothers, had sided   *Seal of Richard I*
with their mother Eleanor when Henry imprisoned her,
and he paid homage to the King of France as his father lay
dying. But when he came to the throne, he saw that he
had misjudged him.

He was tall of stature, and well proportioned, fair and comely of face, of hair bright auburn, of long arms, and nimble in all his joints, high thighs and legs of due proportion, and answerable to the other parts of his body. To speak of his moral parts, his vices for the most part, were but only upon suspicion; incontinency in him much spoken of, nothing proved; but his virtues were apparent, for in all his actions he showed himself valiant, (from whence he had the appellation or surname of Cœur de Lyon) wise, liberal, merciful, just, and which is most of all, religious; a prince born for the good of Christendom; if a bar in his nativity had not hindered it. The remorse for his undutifulness towards his father, was living in him till he died; for at his death he remembered it with bewailing, and desired to be buried as near him as might be, perhaps as thinking they should meet the sooner, that he might ask him forgiveness in another world.

From Sir Richard Baker *A Chronicle of the Kings of England.*

Richard spent only six months of his ten-year reign in England. A renowned warrior – hence his nickname Cœur de Lion – he set out for the Holy Land during the Third Crusade. He reached and took Acre, but had to leave Jerusalem in Saladin's hands. On his return home he was captured by the Duke of Austria, and during his captivity in the castle of Durrenstein he wrote this ballad to his half-sister, Mary of Champagne.

Tomb of Richard I in Fontevrault Abbey

No-one will tell me the cause of my sorrow,
   Why they have made me a prisoner here.
Wherefore with dolour I now make my moan;
   Friends had I many but help have I none.
Shameful it is that they leave me to ransom,
   To languish here two winters long.

*Effigy of
Berengaria of Navarre
in Le Mans Cathedral*

Tomb of John in Worcester Cathedral

John 'Lackland' succeeded to an impoverished crown whose authority had been weakened by the absence of its king. He was forced to concede the Magna Carta to the barons who had the support of the Church and the citizens of London.

He was of stature indifferent tall, and something fat, of a sour and angry countenance, and concerning his conditions, it may be said, that his nature and his fortune did not well agree; for naturally he loved his ease, yet his fortune was to be ever in action. He won more of his enemies by surprises than by battles, which shows he had more of lightning in him than of thunder. He was never so true of his word as

*Tomb of Isabella of Angoulême
in Fontevrault Abbey*

when he threatened, because he meant always as cruelly as
he spake, not always as graciously; and he that would have
known what it was he never meant to perform, must have
looked upon his promises. He was neither fit for prosperity
nor adversity; for prosperity made him insolent, and
adversity dejected; a mean fortune would have suited best
with him. He was all that he was by fits; sometimes doing
nothing without deliberation, and sometimes doing all
upon a sudden; sometimes very religious, and sometimes
scarce a Christian. His insatiableness of money was not so
much as that no man knew what he did with it, gotten
with much noise, but spent in silence. He was but intemperate
in his best temper, but when distempered with a sickness,
most of all, as appeared at his last, when being in a fever he

Manuscript illustration of John at a staghunt

would needs be eating of raw peaches, and drinking of sweet ale. If we look upon his works we must needs think him a worthy prince, but if upon his actions, nothing less; for his works of piety were very many, as hath been showed before, but as for his actions, he neither came to the crown by justice, nor held it with any honour, nor left it in peace. Yet having had many good parts in him, and especially having his royal posterity continued to this day, we can do no less than honour his memory.

From Sir Richard Baker *A Chronicle of the Kings of England.*

Henry III, a cultivated man, reigned for forty years.

He was of stature but mean, yet of a well compacted body,
and very strong; one of his eyelids hanging down, and
almost covering the black of his eye; for his inward
endowments, it may be said, he was wiser for a man, than
for a prince; for he knew better how to govern his life than
his subjects. He was rather pious than devout, as taking
more pleasure in hearing masses than sermons, as he said
to the King of France, he had rather see his friend once,
than hear from him often. His mind seemed not to stand

Effigy of Henry III in
Westminster Abbey

firm upon its basis, for every sudden accident put him into passion. He was neither constant in his love, nor in his hate; for he never had so great a favourite whom he cast not into disgrace, nor so great an enemy whom he received not into favour. An example of both which qualities was seen in his carriage towards Hubert de Burgh, who was for a time his greatest favourite, yet cast out afterward in miserable disgrace, and than no man held in greater hatred, yet received afterward into grace again.

He was more desirous of money than of honour, for else he would never have sold his right to the two great dukedoms of Normandy and Anjou to the King of France for a sum of money. Yet he was more desirous of honour than of quietness, for else he would never have contended so long with his barons about their charter of liberty, which was upon the matter, but a point of honour. His most eminent virtue, and that which made him the more eminent, as being rare in princes, was his continency.

From Sir Richard Baker *A Chronicle of the Kings of England.*

*Stone boss of
Eleanor of Provence in
Bridlington Priory*

Seal of Edward I

T021514

Edward I, whose motto was 'I keep my promise', and whose greatness lay in his attempt to fulfil it, was also known as the Hammer of the Scots. He went far to unifying Britain, and was so impressed by the Welsh use of the longbow that he decreed that archery should be the sole sport permitted to his able-bodied subjects.

He was tall of stature, higher than ordinary men by head and shoulders, and thereof called Longshank; of a swarthy complexion, strong of body, but lean; of a comely favour; his eyes in his anger, sparkling like fire; the hair of his head black and curled. Concerning his conditions, as he was in war peaceful; so in peace he was warlike, delighting specially in that kind of hunting, which is to kill stags or other wild beasts with spears. In continency of life, he was equal to his father; in acts of valour, far beyond him. He had in him the two wisdoms, not often found in any, single; both together, seldom or never: an ability of judgment in himself, and a readiness to hear the judgment of others. He was not easily provoked into passion, but once in passion, not easily appeased, as was seen by his dealing with the Scots; towards whom he showed at first patience, and at last severity. If he be censured for his many taxations, he may be justified by his well bestowing them; for never prince laid out his money to more honour of himself, or good of his kingdom. His great unfortunateness was in his greatest blessing; for of four sons which he had by his wife Queen Eleanor, three of them died in his own life time, who were worthy to have outlived him; and the fourth outlived him, who was worthy never to have been born.

From Sir Richard Baker *A Chronicle of the Kings of England*.

Manuscript illustration showing Edward I at the 'Model' Parliament

Manuscript drawing of
Edward I
Effigy of Eleanor of Castile in
Westminster Abbey

*Stone boss of
Margaret of France in
Winchelsea Church*

Stone boss of Isabella of France in Bristol Cathedral

Edward II was married to Isabella of France shortly after his accession but he seems to have preferred his favourite Piers Gaveston. She later took their son to France against Edward's wishes – hence this letter from father to son.

Edward, fair son,

Inasmuch as it seems, you say, you cannot return to us, because of your mother, it causes us great uneasiness of heart that you cannot be allowed by her to do that which is your natural duty, and which not doing will lead to much mischief.

Fair son, you know how dearly she would have been loved and cherished, if she had timely come, according to her duty to her lord. We have knowledge of much of her evil doings, to our sorrow; how that she openly, notoriously, and knowing it to be contrary to her duty, and against the welfare of our crown, has attached to herself, and retains in her company, the Mortimer, our traitor and mortal foe, proved, attainted, and adjudged, and him she accompanies in the house and abroad, despite of us, of our crown, and the right ordering of the realm – him, the malefactor, whom our beloved brother the King of France, at our request, banished from his dominions as our enemy! And worse than this she has done, if worse than this can be, in allowing you to consort with our said enemy, making him your counsellor, and you openly to herd and associate with him, in the sight of all the world, doing so great a villany and dishonour both to yourself and us, to the prejudice of our crown, and of the laws and customs of our realm, which you are supremely bound to hold, preserve, and maintain.

Wherefore, fair son, desist you from a part which is so shameful. We are not pleased with you; and neither for your mother, nor for any other, ought you to displease us. We charge you that you come to us without opposition, delay, or any further excuse; for your mother has written to us, that if you wish to return to us she will not prevent it.

In no manner, then, either for your mother, nor for any other cause, delay to come to us. Our commands are for your good, and for your honour, by the help of God. Come quickly, then, without further excuse, if you would have our blessing, and avoid our reproach and indignation.

*Effigy of Edward II in
Gloucester Cathedral*

The Queen took Mortimer as her lover and he helped to
force Edward's abdication by blackmailing him over the
safety of his children.

King Edward   Leicester, if gentle words might comfort me,
               Thy speeches long ago had eas'd my sorrows,
               For kind and loving hast thou always been.
               The griefs of private men are soon allay'd;
               But not of Kings. The forest deer, being struck,
               Runs to an herb that closeth up the wounds;
               But when the imperial lion's flesh is gor'd,
               He rends and tears it with his wrathful paw,
               [And] highly scorning that the lowly earth
               Should drink his blood, mounts up into the air:
               And so it fares with me, whose dauntless mind
               Th'ambitious Mortimer would seek to curb,
               And that unnatural Queen, false Isabel,
               That thus hath pent and mew'd me in a prison
               For such outrageous passions cloy my soul,
               As with the wings of rancour and disdain
               Full often am I soaring up to heaven,
               To plain me to the gods against them both.
               But when I call to mind I am a King,
               Methinks I should revenge me of the wrongs,
               That Mortimer and Isabel have done.
               But what are Kings, when regiment is gone,
               But perfect shadows in a sunshine day?
               My nobles rule; I bear the name of King;
               I wear the crown, but am controlled by them,
               By Mortimer, and my unconstant Queen,
               Who spots my nuptial bed with infamy;
               Whilst I am lodged within this cave of care,
               Where sorrow at my elbow still attends.

               From Christopher Marlowe *Edward II.*

After being harried from one prison to another, he was
brutally murdered. His end was the most wretched of
all the English kings.

Thus was king Edward murdered, in the year 1327, on the
22 of September. He was known to be of a good and
courteous nature, though not of most pregnant wit. And
albeit in his youth he fell into certain light crimes, and after
by the company and counsel of evil men, was induced into
more heinous vices, yet was it thought that he purged the
same by repentance. He had surely good cause to repent

*Isabella of France from an
illuminated manuscript*

his former trade of living, for by his indiscreet and wanton misgovernance, there were headed and put to death during his reign (by judgment of law) to the number of 28 barons and knights.

All these mischiefs and many more happened not only to him, but also to the whole state of the realm, in that he wanted judgment and prudent discretion to make choice of sage and discreet counsellors, receiving those into his favour, that abused the same to their private gain and advantage, for which they only sought, insomuch that by their covetous rapine, spoil, and immoderate ambition, the hearts of the common people and nobility were quite estranged from the dutiful love and obedience which they ought to have showed to their sovereign.

But now to make an end of the life as well as of the reign of King Edward the second, I find that after he was deposed of his kingly honour and title, at length they brought him back again in secret manner unto the castle of Berkeley, where whilst he remained (as some write) the Queen would send unto him courteous and loving letters with apparel and other such things, but she would not once come near to visit him, bearing him in hand that she durst not, for fear of the people's displeasure, who hated him so extremely. Howbeit, she with the rest of her confederates had (no doubt) laid the plot of their device for his dispatch, though by painted words she pretended a kind of remorse to him in this his distress.

Whereupon when they saw that such practices would not serve their turn, they came suddenly one night into the chamber where he lay in bed fast asleep, and with heavy featherbeds or a table (as some write) being cast upon him, they kept him down and withal put into his fundament an horn, and through the same they thrust up into his body a hot spit, or (as other have) through the pipe of a trumpet a plumber's instrument of iron made very hot, the which passing up into his entrails, and being rolled to and fro, burnt the same, but so as no appearance of any wound or hurt outwardly might be once perceived. His cry did move many within the castle and town of Berkeley to compassion, plainly hearing him utter a wailful noise, as the tormentors were about to murder him, so that diverse being awakened therewith (as they themselves confessed) prayed heartily to God to receive his soul, when they understood by his cry what the matter meant.

From Rafael Holinshed *Chronicles of England*.

Edward III ascended the throne on his father's abdication.

Effigy of Edward III in Westminster Abbey

This King, besides his other gifts of nature, was aided greatly by his seemly personage. He had a provident wit, sharp to conceive and understand: he was courteous and gentle, a man of great temperance and sobriety, of body well made, of a convenient stature, as neither of the highest nor lowest sort: of face fair and manlike, eyes bright and shining and in age bald, but so as it was rather a seemliness to those his ancient years than any disfiguring to his visage; in knowledge of martial affairs very skilful, as the enterprises and worthy acts by him achieved do sufficiently witness.

Examples of bounteous liberality, and great clemency he shewed many; so that in manner he alone amongst all other kings was found to be one, subject to none, or at the least, to very light and small faults. But yet he was not void of evil haps: for whereas, during the term of forty years' space he reigned in high felicity, and as one happy in all his doings; so in the rest of his time that followed, he felt a wonderful change in fortune. For such is the state of this world, seldom doth prosperity continue, and guide the stern of our worldly doings. For in the first years of his reign, after he once began to govern of himself, he recovered that which had been lost in Scotland, by great victories obtained against his adversaries, subduing the country on each hand, so that he placed governors, and bestowed offices, lands and livings in that realm at his pleasure.

But finally the thing that most grieved him, was the loss of that most noble gentleman, his dear son Prince Edward, in whom was found all parts that might be wished in a worthy governor. But this and other mishaps that chanced to him now in his old years, might seem to come to pass for a revenge of his disobedience showed to his father in usurping against him, although it might be said, that he did it by constraint, and through the advice of others. But whether remorse hereof, or of his other offences moved him, it may seem (as some write) that the consideration of this world's mutability, which he tried to the full, caused him (as is thought) to have in mind the life in the world to come, and therefore of a pure devotion founded the church and college of Saint Stephen at Westminster, and another at Cambridge called the King's Hall.

From Rafael Holinshed *Chronicles of England*.

King Edward III attempts the seduction of the Countess of
Salisbury – an apocryphal story from the Shakespeare
Apocrypha. This passage comes from the anonymous play
of *Edward III* of which parts, including what follows, are
thought by many scholars to have been written by
Shakespeare.

Hast thou pen, ink, and paper ready, Lodowick?	King
Ready, my liege.	Lodowick

Then in the summer arbour sit by me,   King
Make it our counsel-house or cabinet:
Since green our thoughts, green be the conventicle,
Where we will ease us by disburdening them.
Now, Lodowick, invocate some golden Muse,
To bring thee hither an enchanted pen.
And when thou writ'st of tears, encouch the word
Before and after with such sweet laments,
That it may raise drops in a Tartar's eye,
And make a flintheart Scythian pitiful.

To whom, my Lord, shall I direct my style?   Lodowick

To one that shames the fair and sots the wise;   King
Whose body is an abstract or a brief,
Contains each general virtue in the world.
Better than beautiful thou must begin,
Devise for fair a fairer word than fair,
And every ornament that thou would'st praise,
Fly it a pitch above the soar of praise.
Begin; I will to contemplate the while:
Forget not to set down, how passionate,
How heart-sick, and how full of languishment
Her beauty makes me.

Write I to a woman?   Lodowick

What, think'st thou I did bid thee praise a horse?   King

Of what condition or estate she is,   Lodowick
'Twere requisite that I should know, my Lord.

King   Of such estate, that hers is as a throne,
And my estate the footstool, where she treads:
Write on, while I peruse her in my thoughts.
Her voice to music or the nightingale –
To music every summer leaping swain
Compares his sunburnt lover when she speaks;
And why should I speak of the nightingale?
The nightingale sings of adulterate wrong,
And that, compared, is too satirical.
Her hair, far softer than the silk-worm's twist,
Like to a flattering glass, doth make more fair
The yellow amber: – like a flattering glass
Comes in too soon; for, writing of her eyes,
I'll say that like a glass they catch the sun,
And thence the hot reflexion doth rebound
Against my breast, and burns my heart within.
Ah, what a world of descant makes my soul
Upon this voluntary ground of love! –
Come, Lodowick, hast thou turn'd thy ink to gold?
Read, Lord, read;
Fill thou the empty hollows of mine ears
With the sweet hearing of thy poetry.

Lodowick   'More fair and chaste then is the queen of shades,' –

King   That line hath two faults, gross and palpable:
Compar'st thou her to the pale queen of night,
Who, being set in dark, seems therefore light?
What is she, when the sun lifts up his head,
But like a fading taper, dim and dead?

Lodowick   What is the other fault, my sovereign lord?

King   Read o'er the line again.

Lodowick   'More fair and chaste' –

King   I did not bid thee talk of chastity,
To ransack so the treasure of her mind;
For I had rather have her chas'd than chaste.
Out with the moon line, I will none of it;
And let me have her liken'd to the sun;
Say she hath thrice more splendour than the sun,
That her perfections emulate the sun,
That she breeds sweets as plenteous as the sun,
That she doth thaw cold winter like the sun,
That she doth cheer fresh summer like the sun,

That she doth dazzle gazers like the sun;
And, in this application to the sun,
Bid her be free and general as the sun,
Who smiles upon the basest weed that grows
As lovingly as on the fragrant rose.
Let's see what follows that same moonlight line.

'More fair and chaste then is the queen of shades,   Lodowick
More bold in constancy' –

In constancy! than who?   King

'Than Judith was.'   Lodowick

O monstrous line! Put in the next a sword,   King
And I shall woo her to cut off my head.
Blot, blot, good Lodowick! Let us hear the next.

There's all that yet is done.   Lodowick

I thank thee, then; thou hast done little ill,   King
But what is done, is passing, passing ill.
No, let the Captain talk of boistrous war,
The prisoner of immured dark constraint,
The sick man best sets down the pangs of death,
The man that starves the sweetness of a feast,
The frozen soul the benefit of fire,
And every grief his happy opposite:
Love cannot sound well but in lovers' tongues;
Give me the pen and paper, I will write.

Edward's wantonness was kept in check by his devotion to his wife Philippa of Hainault. After her death he became besotted by Alice Perrers, who is reputed to have stripped his dead body of all its jewellery.

After the Parliament, the King, whom excessive impairment of old age had oppressed for a long time, rapidly became more troubled. For he fell into a weakness not of the kind which is believed to be usual in old men, but which is said to attach itself for the most part to youths given to lechery. But the cure of that disease is far more difficult in an old man than in a young one, for the different reasons of the old man's chilliness and the young man's heat. And, therefore, the Lord King was weakened the more because the natural fluid and nutritive heat in him were now almost exhausted, and his virility failed. In truth it is said by many that he developed this disorder owing to his desire for that wanton baggage Alice Perrers, who had been kept from his presence. This was proved later on, for he took Alice back into their old relation. During this time the King's weakness increased, and he began to be despaired of by his physicians, although the before-mentioned courtesan along with her daughter Isabella had lain with him all night long.

At Christmas the King was at Havering-at-Bower, where he was then much troubled by the great impairment of his body. On May 22nd he began to show signs of death, by which his attendants, and indeed he himself, knew that he was about to die. And quite a short time after he returned his soul to God.

From an unknown chronicler.

*Effigy of Philippa of Hainault
in Westminster Abbey*

Portrait of Richard II

Richard of Bordeaux was the son of the Black Prince.
A man of great cultivation, he preferred the niceties of life
to its realities. (He is credited with the invention of the
handkerchief.) He was deposed and murdered by his cousin,
Henry Bolingbroke, Duke of Lancaster and Earl of Derby.

In the mean season while the King sat at dinner, who did
eat but little, his heart was so full that he had no lust to eat,
all the country about the castle was full of men of war.
Then he demanded of his cousin what men they were that
appeared so many in the fields. "What would they have?"
quoth the King. "They will have you," quoth the Earl,
"and bring you to London, and put you in the Tower; there
is no other remedy, you can escape not otherwise."

"No," quoth the King, and he was sore afraid of those
words, and said, "Cousin, can you not provide for my surety?
I will not gladly put me in their hands for I know well they
hate me and have done long, though I be their King." Then
the Earl said, "Sir, I see no other remedy but to yield
yourself as my prisoner; and when they know that you be
my prisoner they will do you no hurt; but you must so
ordain you and your company to ride to London with me,
and to be as my prisoner in the Tower of London."

The King, who saw himself in a hard case, all his spirits
were sore abashed as he doubted greatly that the Londoners
would slay him. Then he yielded himself prisoner to the
Earl of Derby and bound himself, and promised to do all
that he would have him do.

The Earl then ordained incontinent horses to be saddled
and brought forth into the court and the gates opened.
Then many men of arms and archers entered. Then the

Earl of Derby caused a cry to be made; on pain of death no man to be so hardy as to take away anything within the castle nor to lay any hands upon any person, for all were under the Earl's safeguard and protection, which cry was kept, no man dared break it.

While everything was a-preparing, the King and the Earl communed together in the court. And as I was informed, King Richard had a greyhound called Matt, who always waited upon the King, and would know no man else. For whensoever the King did ride, he that kept the greyhound did let him loose, and he would straight run to the King and fawn upon him, and leap with his forefeet upon the King's shoulders. And as the King and the Earl of Derby talked together in the court, the greyhound, who was wont to leap upon the King, left the King and came to the Earl of Derby, Duke of Lancaster, and made to him the same friendly countenance and cheer as he was wont to do to the King. The Duke, who knew not the greyhound, demanded of the King what the greyhound would do. "Cousin," quoth the King, "it is a great good token to you, and an evil sign to me."

"Sir, how know you that?" quoth the Duke. "I know it well," quoth the King; "the greyhound makes you cheer this day as King of England, as you shall be, and I shall be deposed: the greyhound has this knowledge naturally; therefore take him to you, he will follow you and forsake me." The Duke understood well those words, and cherished the greyhound, who would never after follow King Richard but followed the Duke of Lancaster.

From Sir John Froissart *Chronicles.*

Effigy of Anne of Bohemia

Henry's guilt concerning Richard's murder was never to leave him.

Henry   Thou has heard that King Richard is alive, and art glad thereof.

Friar   I am glad as a man is glad of the life of his friend, for I am holden to him, and all my kin, for he was our furtherer and promoter.

Henry   Thou hast noised and told openly that he liveth and so hast excited and stirred the people against me.

Friar   Nay.

Henry   Tell me truth as it is in thy heart: if thou sawest King Richard and me in a field fighting together, with whom wouldest thou hold?

Friar   Forsooth, with him, for I am more beholden to him.

Henry   Thou wouldest that I and all the lords of my realm were dead?

Friar   Nay.

Henry   What wouldest thou do with me if thou haddest the victory over me?

Friar   I would make you Duke of Lancaster.

Henry   Thou art not my friend, and therefore thou shalt lose thy head.

From an unknown chronicler.

The Coronation of Henry IV

King Henry   How many thousand of my poorest subjects
Are at this hour asleep! O sleep, O gentle sleep,
Nature's soft nurse, how have I frighted thee,
That thou no more wilt weigh my eyelids down,
And steep my senses in forgetfulness?
Why rather, sleep, liest thou in smoky cribs,
Upon uneasy pallets stretching thee,
And hush'd with buzzing night-flies to thy slumber,
Than in the perfum'd chambers of the great,
Under the canopies of costly state,
And lull'd with sound of sweetest melody?
O thou dull god, why liest thou with the vile
In loathsome beds, and leav'st the kingly couch
A watch-case or a common 'larum-bell?
Wilt thou upon the high and giddy mast
Seal up the ship-boy's eyes, and rock his brains
In cradle of the rude imperious surge
And in the visitation of the winds,
Who take the ruffian billows by the top,
Curling their monstrous heads, and hanging them
With deafing clamour in the slippery clouds,
That, with the hurly, death itself awakes?
Canst thou, O partial sleep, give thy repose
To the wet sea-boy in an hour so rude;
And in the calmest and most stillest night,
With all appliances and means to boot,
Deny it to a king? Then, happy low, lie down!
Uneasy lies the head that wears a crown.

From William Shakespeare *Henry IV*.

**Shakespeare found Rafael Holinshed a useful source and
stuck closely to his account in his chronicles.**

During his last sickness, he caused his crown (as some write)
to be set on a pillow at his bed's head, and suddenly his
pangs so sore troubled him, that he lay as though all his
vital spirits had been from him departed. Such as were
about him, thinking verily that he had been departed,
covered his face with a linen cloth.

The Prince his son being hereof advertised, entered into
the chamber, took away the crown, and departed. The
father being suddenly revived out of that trance, quickly
perceived the lack of his crown; and having knowledge that

*Effigy of Henry IV and Joan of
Navarre in Canterbury
Cathedral*

the Prince his son had taken it away, caused him to come before his presence, requiring of him what he meant so to misuse himself. The Prince with a good audacity answered; 'Sir, to mine and all men's judgments you seemed dead in this world, wherefore I as your next heir apparent took that as mine own, and not as yours.' Well fair son (said the King with a great sigh) what right I had to it, God knoweth. Well (said the Prince) if you die King, I will have the garland, and trust to keep it with the sword against all mine enemies as you have done. Then said the King, 'I commit all to God, and remember you to do well.'

We find, that he was taken with his last sickness, while he was making his prayers at Saint Edward's shrine, there as it were to take his leave, and so to proceed forth on his journey: he was so suddenly and grievously taken, that such as were about him, feared lest he would have died presently, wherefore to relieve him (if it were possible) they bare him into a chamber that was next at hand, belonging to the Abbot of Westminster, where they laid him on a pallet before the fire, and used all remedies to revive him. At length, he recovered his speech, and understanding and perceiving himself in a strange place which he knew not, he willed to know if the chamber had any particular name, whereunto answer was made, that it was called Jerusalem. Then said the King; 'Lauds be given to the father of heaven, for now I know that I shall die here in this chamber, according to the prophecy of me declared, that I should depart this life in Jerusalem.'

This King was of a mean stature, well proportioned, and formally compact, quick and lively, and of a stout courage. In his later days he showed himself so gentle, that he got more love amongst the nobles and people of this realm, than he had purchased malice and evil will in the beginning.

But yet to speak a truth, by his proceedings, after he had attained to the crown, what with such taxes, tallages, subsidies, and exactions as he was constrained to charge the people with; and what by punishing such as moved with disdain to see him usurp the crown, did at sundry times rebel against him, he won himself more hatred, than in all his life time (if it had been longer by many years than it was) had been possible for him to have weeded out and removed. And yet doubtless, worthy were his subjects to taste of that bitter cup, sithens they were so ready to join and clap hands with him, for the deposing of their rightful and natural prince King Richard, whose chief fault rested only in that, that he was too bountiful to his friends, and too merciful to his foes.

Entre fut et est̃
Je fux ichan frois
fart pour œ tampe
le louier et chunoine de chynay

Jane Austen, at the age of fifteen, wrote a short and characteristically high-spirited history of the English kings entitled 'The History of England' by a Partial, Prejudiced and Ignorant Historian. She started with Henry IV.

Henry IV's signature on an Exchequer Roll

Henry the 4th ascended the throne of England much to his own satisfaction in the year 1399, after having prevailed on his cousin and predecessor Richard the 2nd, to resign it to him, and to retire for the rest of his life to Pomfret Castle, where he happened to be murdered. It is to be supposed that Henry was married, since he had certainly four sons, but it is not in my power to inform the Reader who was his wife. Be this as it may, he did not live for ever, but falling ill, his son the Prince of Wales came and took away the crown; whereupon the King made a long speech, for which I must refer the Reader to Shakespear's Plays, and the Prince made a still longer. Things being thus settled between them the King died, and was succeeded by his son Henry.

Portrait of Henry V

Henry V, popularly thought of as one of England's great hero kings, was nevertheless a ruthless tough. His concept of war was more akin to that of later ages and earned him a hard reputation abroad.

This Henry was a king, of life without spot, a prince whom all men loved, and of none disdained, a captain against whom fortune never frowned, nor mischance once spurned, whose people him so severe a justicer both loved and obeyed (and so humane withal) that he left no offence unpunished, nor friendship unrewarded; a terror to rebels, and suppressor of sedition, his virtues notable, his qualities most praiseworthy.

In strength and nimbleness of body from his youth few were comparable to him, for in wrestling, leaping, and running, no man well able to compare. In casting of great iron bars and heavy stones he excelled commonly all men, never shrinking at cold, nor slothful for heat; and when he most laboured, his head commonly uncovered; no more weary of harness than a light cloak, very valiantly abiding at need both hunger and thirst; so manful of mind as never seen to quinch at a wound, or to smart at the pain; nor to turn his nose from evil savour, nor close his eyes from smoke or dust; no man more moderate in eating and drinking, with diet not delicate, but rather more meat for men of war, than for princes, or tender stomachs. Every honest person was permitted to come to him, sitting at meal, where either secretly or openly to declare his mind. High and weighty causes as well between men of war and other he would gladly hear, and either determined them himself, or else, for end committed them to others. He slept very little, but that very soundly, in so much that when his soldiers sang at nights, or minstrels played, he then slept fastest; of courage invincible, of purpose immutable, so wisehardy always, as fear was banished from him; at every alarum he first in armour and foremost in ordering. In time of war such was his providence, bounty and hap, as he had true intelligence not only what his enemies did, but what they said and intended; of his devices and purposes few; before the thing was at the point to be done, should be made privy.

He had such knowledge in ordering and guiding an army, with such a gift to encourage his people, that the Frenchmen had constant opinion he could never be

vanquished in battle. Such wit, such prudence, and such policy withal, that he never enterprised any thing, before he had fully debated and forecast all the main chances that might happen, which done with all diligence and courage he set his purpose forward. What policy he had in finding present remedies for sudden mischiefs, and what engines in saving himself and his people in sharp distresses: were it not that by his acts they did plainly appear, hard were it by words to make them credible. Wantonness of life and thirst in avarice had he quite quenched in him; virtues indeed in such an estate of sovereignty, youth, and power, as very rare, so right commendable in the highest degree. So staid of mind and countenance beside, that never jolly or triumphant for victory, nor sad or damped for loss or misfortune. For bountifulness and liberality, no man more free, gentle, and frank, in bestowing rewards to all persons, according to their deserts: for his saying was, that he never desired money to keep but to give and spend.

From Rafael Holinshed *Chronicles of England*.

King Henry	Upon the king! Let us our lives, our souls,
	Our debts, our careful wives,
	Our children, and our sins, lay on the king!
	We must bear all. O hard condition,
	Twin-born with greatness, subject to the breath
	Of every fool, whose sense no more can feel
	But his own wringing! What infinite heart's ease
	Must kings neglect, that private men enjoy!
	And what have kings that privates have not too,
	Save ceremony – save general economy?
	And what art thou, thou idol ceremony?
	What kind of god art thou, that suffer'st more
	Of mortal griefs than do thy worshippers?
	What are thy rents? What are thy coming-in?
	O Ceremony, show me but thy worth!
	What is thy soul of adoration?
	Art thou aught else but place, degree and form,
	Creating awe and fear in other men?
	Wherein thou art less happy being fear'd
	Than they in fearing.
	What drink'st thou oft, instead of homage sweet,
	But poison'd flattery? O, be sick, great greatness,
	And bid thy ceremony give thee cure!
	Think'st thou the fiery fever will go out

Henry V's helmet, saddle and shield

The marriage of Henry V to Catherine of France from a manuscript drawing

With titles blown from adulation?
Will it give place to flexure and low bending?
Can'st thou, when thou command'st the beggar's knee,
Command the health of it? No, thou proud dream,
That play'st so subtly with a king's repose.
I am a king that find thee, and I know
'Tis not the balm, the sceptre and the ball,
The sword, the mace, the crown imperial,
The intertissued robe of gold and pearl,
The farced title running 'fore the king.
The throne he sits on, nor the tide of pomp
That beats upon the high shore of this world,
No, not all these, thrice-gorgeous ceremony,
Not all these, laid in bed majestical,
Can sleep so soundly as the wretched slave,
Who with a body fill'd and vacant mind
Gets him to rest, cramm'd with distressful bread;
Never sees horrid night, the child of hell,
But, like a lackey, from the rise to set
Sweats in the eye of Phoebus and all night
Sleeps in Elysium; next day after dawn,
Doth rise and help Hyperion to his horse,
And follows so the ever-running year,
With profitable labour, to his grave:
And, but for ceremony, such a wretch,
Winding up days with toil and nights with sleep,
Had the fore-hand and vantage of a king.

From William Shakespeare *Henry V*.

This prince after he succeeded to the throne grew quite reformed and amiable, forsaking all his dissipated companions. His Majesty then turned his thoughts to France, where he went and fought the famous Battle of Agincourt. He afterwards married the King's daughter Catherine, a very agreeable woman by Shakespear's account. In spite of all this however he died, and was succeeded by his son Henry.

From Jane Austen.

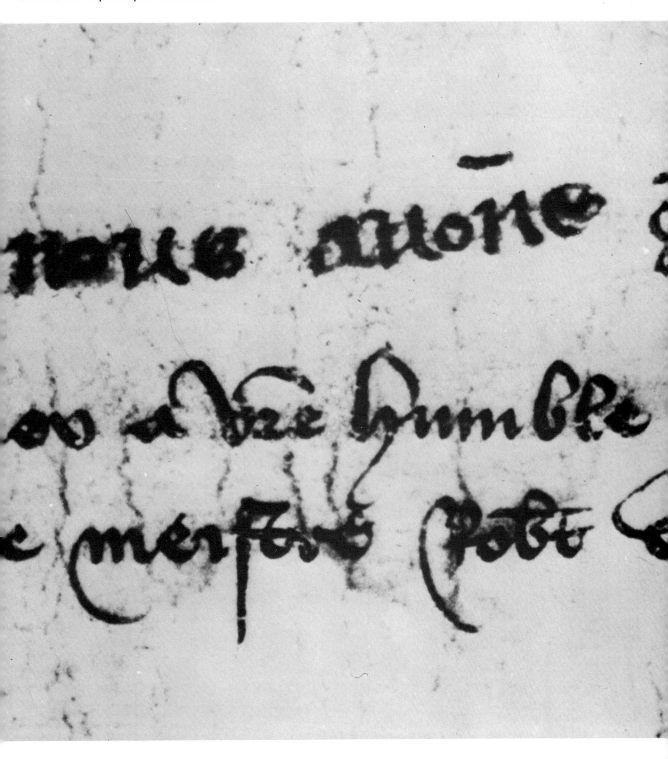

Henry VI of Lancaster came to the throne as a year-old
baby in 1422. His precarious tenure lasted until 1461
when Edward IV of York seized him and it.

Henry VI's signature
from an Exchequer Roll

He was a man of pure simplicity of mind, truthful almost to a fault. He never made a promise he did not keep, never knowingly did an injury to any one. Rectitude and justice ruled his conduct in all public affairs. Devout himself, he sought to cherish a love for religion in others. He would exhort his visitors, particularly the young to pursue virtue and eschew evil. He considered sports and the pleasures of the world as frivolous, and devoted his leisure to reading the Scriptures and the old Chronicles. Most decorous himself when attending public worship, he obliged his courtiers to enter the sacred edifice without swords or spears, and to refrain from interrupting the devotion of others by conversing within its precincts.

He delighted in female society, and blamed that immodest dress, which left exposed the maternal parts of the neck. 'Fie, fie, for shame!' he exclaimed, 'forsooth ye be to blame.' Fond of encouraging youth in the path of virtue he would frequently converse familiarly with the scholars from his college of Eton, when they visited his servants at Windsor Castle. He generally concluded with this address, adding a present of money: 'Be good lads, meek and docile, and attend to your religion.'

He was liberal to the poor, and lived among his dependants as a father among his children. He readily forgave those who had offended him. When one of his servants had been robbed, he sent him a present of twenty nobles, desiring him to be more careful of his property in future, and requesting him to forgive the thief. Passing one day from St Albans to Cripplegate, he saw a quarter of a man impaled there for treason. Greatly shocked he exclaimed: 'Take it away, take it away, I will have no man so cruelly treated on my account.' Hearing that four men of noble birth were about to suffer for treason to him, he sent them his pardon with all expedition to the place of execution.

In his dress he was plain, and would not wear the shoes with the upturned points, then so much in fashion, and considered the distinguishing mark of a man of quality. Where are warm baths in which they say the men of that country customarily refresh and wash themselves, the King, looking into the baths, saw in them men wholly naked with every garment cast off. At which he was greatly displeased, and went away quickly, abhorring such nudity as a great

offence and not unmindful of that sentence of Francis
Petrarch 'the nakedness of a beast is in men unpleasing, but
the decency of raiment makes for modesty'.

From John Blakman.

**Henry VI was married to the daughter of René of Anjou; a
woman of strong character, she espoused her husband's
Lancastrian cause and never lost a battle until her defeat
at Tewkesbury in 1470. But for her Henry might have
come to terms with the Yorkists. Arriving in England at
the age of sixteen, she gives no hint of her later spirit and
courage.**

I am writing to report what an Englishman told me about
the magnificence of the Queen of England and how she was
brought to England. I will tell you something of the King of
England. First of all the Englishman told me that the King
of England took her without a dowry and he even restored
some lands which he held to her father. When the Queen
landed in England the King dressed himself as a squire, the
duke of Suffolk doing the same, and took her a letter which
he said the King of England had written. When the Queen
read the letter the King took stock of her, saying that a
woman may be seen over well when she reads a letter, and
the Queen never found that it was the King, because she
was so engrossed in reading the letter, and she never
looked at the King, in his squire's dress, who remained on
his knees all the time. After the King had gone, the duke of
Suffolk said: 'Most serene Queen, what do you think of the
squire who brought you the letter?' The Queen replied: 'I
did not notice him, as I was occupied in reading the letter he
brought.' The duke remarked: 'Most serene Queen, the
person dressed as a squire was the most serene King of
England,' and the Queen was vexed at not having known it,
because she had kept him on his knees.

From a letter by Raffaelo de Negra, a Venetian envoy.

*Medal showing Margaret of
Anjou by Pietro da Milano
Portrait of Henry VI*

Shakespeare catches the King's vacillation and
unworldliness.

*The marriage of Henry VI to
Margaret of Anjou from a
manuscript illumination*

King Henry

Here on this molehill will I sit me down.
To whom God will, there be the victory!
For Margaret my queen, and Clifford too,
Have chid me from the battle; swearing both
They prosper best of all when I am thence.
Would I were dead, if God's good will were so!
For what is in this world but grief and woe?
O God! methinks it were a happy life
To be no better than a homely swain;
To sit upon a hill, as I do now,
To carve out dials quaintly, point by point,
Thereby to see the minutes how they run,
How many make the hour full complete;
How many hours bring about the day;
How many days will finish up the year;
How many years a mortal man may live.
When this is known, then to divide the times:
So many hours must I tend my flock;
So many hours must I take my rest;
So many hours must I contemplate;
So many hours must I sport myself;
So many days my ewes have been with young;
So many weeks ere the poor fools will ean;
So many years ere I shall shear the fleece:
So minutes, hours, days, months, and years,
Pass'd over to the end they were created,
Would bring white hairs unto a quiet grave.
Ah, what a life were this! how sweet! how lovely!
Gives not the hawthorn-bush a sweeter shade
To shepherds looking on their silly sheep,
Than doth a rich embroider'd canopy
To kings that fear their subjects' treachery?
O, yes, it doth; a thousand-fold it doth.
And to conclude, the shepherd's homely curds,
His cold thin drink out of his leather bottle,
His wonted sleep under a fresh tree's shade,
All which secure and sweetly he enjoys,
Is far beyond a prince's delicates,
His viands sparkling in a golden cup,
His body couched in a curious bed,
When care, mistrust, and treason waits on him.

From William Shakespeare *Henry VI.*

But even his wife's fighting spirit could not keep him out of the Tower of London where he spent five years, from 1464–69. He wrote this poem there.

> Kingdoms are but cares,
>   State is devoid of stay,
> Riches are ready snares,
>   and hasten to decay.

> Pleasure is a privy prick
>   Which vice doth still provoke;
> Pomp, imprompt; and fame, a flame;
>   Power, a smouldering smoke.

> Who meaneth to remove the rock
>   Out of the slimy mud,
> Shall mire himself, and hardly 'scape
>   The swelling of the flood.

I cannot say much for this Monarch's sense. Nor would I if I could, for he was a Lancastrian. I suppose you know all about the Wars between him and the Duke of York who was of the right side; if you do not, you had better read some other History, for I shall not be very diffuse in this, meaning by it only to vent my spleen against, and shew my Hatred to all those people whose parties or principles do not suit with mine, and not to give information. This King married Margaret of Anjou, a Woman whose distresses and misfortunes were so great as almost to make me who hate her, pity her. It was in this reign that Joan of Arc lived and made such a row among the English. They should not have burnt her – but they did. There were several Battles between the Yorkists and Lancastrians in which the former (as they ought) usually conquered. At length they were entirely overcome; the King was murdered – The Queen was sent home – and Edward the 4th ascended the Throne.

From Jane Austen.

Edward IV first became king at the age of nineteen but played box and cox with Henry VI. He ruled again from 1471 to 1483, having successfully vanquished Henry's wife, Margaret.

Portrait of Edward IV

He was a goodly personage and very princely to behold; of heart courageous, politic in counsel, in adversity nothing abashed, in prosperity rather joyful than proud, in peace just and merciful, in war sharp and fierce, in the field bold and hardy, and nevertheless no further than wisdom would, adventurous. Whoso well consider his wars, shall no less commend his wisdom where he withdrew than his manhood where he vanquished. He was of visage lovely; of body mighty, strong and clean made; howbeit in his latter days, with over liberal diet, somewhat corpulent and burly but nevertheless not uncomely. He was in youth greatly given to fleshly wantonness, from which health of body in great prosperity and fortune, without a special grace, hardly refrains.

From Sir Thomas More *History of King Richard III.*

*Elizabeth Woodville from a
window in Canterbury
Cathedral*

In May 1464, when he was twenty-two, Edward married
much beneath him. His wooing of Elizabeth Woodville
was blunt and to the point.

King Edward	Brother of Gloucester, at Saint Alban's field This lady's husband, Sir Richard Grey, was slain, His lands then seized on by the conqueror: Her suit is now to repossess those lands.
Gloucester	Your Highness shall do well to grant her suit; It were dishonour to deny it her.
King Edward	It were no less; but yet I'll make a pause.
Gloucester *aside*	Yea, is it so? I see the lady hath a thing to grant, Before the King will grant her humble suit.
Clarence *aside*	He knows the game: how true he keeps the wind!
King Edward	Widow, we will consider of your suit; And come some other time to know our mind.
Lady Grey	Right gracious lord, I cannot brook delay. May it please your Highness to resolve me now; And what your pleasure is shall satisfy me.
Gloucester *aside*	Ay, widow? Then I'll warrant you all your lands, An if what pleases him shall pleasure you.
King Edward	Lords, give us leave: I'll try this widow's wit.

(*Gloucester and Clarence retire*)

King Edward	Now tell me, madam, do you love your children?
Lady Grey	Ay, full as dearly as I love myself.
King Edward	And would you not do much to do them good?
Lady Grey	To do them good, I would sustain some harm.
King Edward	Then get your husband's lands, to do them good.
Lady Grey	Therefore I came unto your Majesty.

King Edward	I'll tell you how these lands are to be got.
Lady Grey	So shall you bind me to your Highness's service.
King Edward	What service wilt thou do me, if I give them?
Lady Grey	What you command that rests in me to do.
King Edward	But you will take exceptions to my boon.
Lady Grey	No, gracious lord, except I cannot do it.
King Edward	Ay, but thou canst do what I mean to ask.
Lady Grey	Why, then I will do what your Grace commands.
Gloucester *aside*	He plies her hard; and much rain wears the marble.
Clarence *aside*	As red as fire! Nay, then her wax must melt.
Lady Grey	Why stops my lord? Shall I not hear my task?
King Edward	An easy task; 'tis but to love a king.
Lady Grey	That's soon performed, because I am a subject.
King Edward	Why, then, thy husband's lands I freely give thee.
Lady Grey	I take my leave with many thousand thanks.
King Edward	But stay thee, 'tis the fruits of love I mean.
Lady Grey	The fruits of love I mean, my loving liege.
King Edward	Ay, but, I fear me, in another sense. What love, think'st thou, I sue so much to get?
Lady Grey	My love till death, my humble thanks, my prayers; That love which virtue begs and virtue grants.
King Edward	No, by my troth, I did not mean such love.
Lady Grey	Why, then you mean not as I thought you did.
King Edward	To tell thee plain, I aim to lie with thee.

To tell thee plain, I had rather lie in prison.   Lady Grey

Why, then thou shalt not have thy husband's lands.   King Edward

But, mighty lord, this merry inclination   Lady Grey
Accords not with the sadness of my suit.
Please you dismiss me, either with ay or no.

Ay, if thou wilt say ay to my request;   King Edward
No, if thou dost say no to my demand.

Then, no, my lord. My suit is at an end.   Lady Grey

The widow likes him not; she knits her brows.   Gloucester
                                                                         aside

He is the bluntest wooer in Christendom.   Clarence
                                                                         aside

Say that King Edward take thee for his queen?   King Edward

'Tis better said than done, my gracious lord.   Lady Grey
I am a subject fit to jest withal,
But far unfit to be a sovereign.

I speak no more than what my soul intends;   King Edward
And that is to enjoy thee for my love.

And that is more than I will yield unto: Lady Grey
I know I am too mean to be your queen,
And yet too good to be your concubine.

You cavil, widow: I did mean my queen.   King Edward

'Twill grieve your Grace my sons should call you father.   Lady Grey

No more than when my daughters call thee mother.   King Edward
Thou art a widow, and thou hast some children;
And, by God's Mother, I, being but a bachelor,
Have other some. Why, 'tis a happy thing
To be the father unto many sons.
Answer no more, for thou shalt be my queen.

The ghostly father now hath done his shrift.   Gloucester

When he was made a shriver, 'twas for shift.   Clarence

King Edward	Brothers, you muse what chat we two have had.
Gloucester	The widow likes it not, for she looks very sad.
King Edward	You'd think it strange if I should marry her.
Clarence	To whom, my lord?
King Edward	Why, Clarence, to myself.
Gloucester	That would be ten days' wonder at the least.
Clarence	That's a day longer than a wonder lasts.
Gloucester	By so much is the wonder in extremes.
King Edward	Well, jest on, brothers: I can tell you both Her suit is granted for her husband's lands.

From William Shakespeare *Henry VI*.

This Monarch was famous only for his Beauty and his Courage, of which the Picture we have here given of him, and his undaunted Behaviour in marrying one Woman while he was engaged to another, are sufficient proofs. His Wife was Elizabeth Woodville, a Widow who, poor Woman! was afterwards confined in a Convent by that Monster of Iniquity and Avarice Henry the 7th. One of Edward's Mistresses was Jane Shore, who had had a play written about her, but it is a tragedy and therefore not worth reading. Having performed all these noble actions, his Majesty died, and was succeeded by his son.

From Jane Austen.

Edward V reigned for only two months. He was thirteen
when he succeeded to the throne. He took his coronation
seriously, as befitted a monarch, but he did not live to
attend it.

Trusty and well-beloved, we greet you well; and by the
advice of our dearest uncle, the Duke of Gloucester,
Protector of this our realm during our young age, and of
the Lords of our Council, we write to you at this time,
willing and nevertheless charging you to prepare and
furnish yourself to receive the noble order of knighthood at
our coronation; which, by God's grace, we intend shall be
solemnised the 22nd day of this present month at our palace
of Westminster, commanding you to be here at our Tower
of London, four days before our said coronation, to have
communication with commissioners concerning that
matter; not failing hereof in any wise, as you intend to
please us, and as he will answer.

From a letter by the King to Otes Gilbert, Squire.

Manuscript portrayal of
Edward V with Richard, Duke
of Gloucester and Anne Neville

Portrait of Richard III

Although the dispute still rages as to whether Richard, Duke of Gloucester, murdered the two princes in the Tower there is no doubt that without the death of Edward V he could not have seized the throne.

But after Hastings was removed, all the attendants who had waited upon the King were debarred access to him. He and his brothers were withdrawn into the inner apartments of the Tower proper, and day by day began to be seen more rarely behind the bars and windows, till at length they ceased to appear altogether. Dr Argentine, the last of his attendants whose services the King enjoyed, reported that the young King, like a victim prepared for sacrifice, sought remission of his sins by daily confession and penance, believing his death to be near at hand. I must not stay silent as touching on the gifts of the youth. In word and deed he gave so many proofs of his liberal education, of gentle, nay rather scholarly, attainments far beyond his age; all of these should be recounted, but require such labour, that I shall lawfully excuse myself the attempt. There is one thing I shall not omit, and that is, his special knowledge of literature, which enabled him to discourse elegantly, to understand fully, and to declaim most excellently from any work whether in verse or prose that came into his hands, unless it were from among the more recondite authors. He had such dignity in his whole person, and in his face such charm, that however much they might gaze they never wearied the eyes of the beholders. I have seen many men burst forth into tears and lamentations when mention was made of him after his removal from men's sight; and already there was a suspicion that he had been murdered. Whether, however, he has been murdered, and by what manner of death, so far I have not at all discovered.

From Dominicus Mancinus.

This unfortunate Prince lived so little a while that nobody had him to draw his picture. He was murdered by his Uncle's Contrivance, whose name was Richard the 3rd.

From Jane Austen.

RICARDVS · III · ANG · REX

The character of Richard III, the last of the Plantagenets, has been the subject of more speculation than that of any other English king. There have been few Yorkist historians to uphold his merits, and Sir Thomas More, anxious to please his Tudor master, started a campaign of vilification that did not end until, in the eighteenth century, Horace Walpole, not very convincingly, took up the cudgels on Richard's behalf.

As he was small and little of stature, so was he of body greatly deformed; the one shoulder higher than the other, his face small but his countenance was cruel, and such, that a man at the first aspect would judge it to savor and smell of malice, fraud and deceit; when he stood musing he would bite and chew basely his nether lip, as who say'd, that his fierce nature in his cruel body always chafed, stirred and was ever unquiet; beside that, the dagger that he wore he would when he studied with his hand pluck up and down in the sheath to the middle, never drawing it fully out, his wit pregnant, quick and ready, wryly to feign and apt to dissimulate, he had a proud mind and an arrogant stomach, the which accompanied him to his death, which he rather desiring to suffer by dent of sword, then being forsaken and destitute of his untrue companions, would by coward flight preserve and save his uncertain life; which by malice, sickness and condign punishment might chance shortly after to come to confusion.

From Hall *Chronicle*.

In the mean season, the dead corpse of King Richard was as shamefully carried to the town of Leicester as he gorgeously the day before with pomp and pride departed out of the same town. For his body was naked and despoiled to the skin, and nothing left about him not so much as a clout to cover his privy members, and was trussed behind a Pursuivant of arms called *Blaunche Senglier* or white Boar, like a Hog or a Calf, the head and arms hanging on the one side of the horse, and the legs on the other side, and all by sprinkled with mire and blood, was brought to the grey Friars Church within the town, and there lay like a miserable spectacle: but surely considering his mischievous acts and ungracious doings, men may worthily wonder at such a captive, and in the said Church he was with no less funeral pomp and solemnity interred, then he would to be done at the burying of his innocent Nephews, whom he caused cruelly to be murdered, and unnaturally to be quelled.

When his death was known, few lamented, and many rejoiced, the proud bragging white Boar (which was his badge) was violently razed and plucked down from every sign and place where it might be espied, so ill was his life, that men wished the memory of him to be buried with his carrion corpse: He reigned two years, two months, and one day.

Thus ended this Prince his mortal life with infamy and dishonour, which never preferred fame or honesty, before ambition, tyranny, and mischief. And if he had continued still Protector, and suffered his nephews to have lived and reigned, no doubt but the Realm had prospered, and he much praised and beloved, as he is now abhorred and despised.

From Grafton *Chronicle.*

*Manuscript portrayal of
Richard III and Anne Neville*

With regard to the person of Richard, it appears to have been as much misrepresented as his actions. The truth I take to have been this. Richard, who was slender and not tall, had one shoulder a little higher than the other; a defect by the magnifying classes of party, by distance of time, and by the amplification of tradition, easily swelled to shocking deformity; for falsehood itself generally pays so much respect to truth as to make it the basis of its superstructures.

In short, that Henry's character, as we have received it from his own apologists, is so much worse and more hateful than Richard's, that we may well believe Henry invented and propagated by far the greater part of the slanders against Richard: that Henry, not Richard, probably put to death the true Duke of York, as he did the Earl of Warwick: and that we are not certain whether Edward the Fifth was murdered; nor, if he was, by whose order he was murdered. For my own part, I know not what to think of the death of Edward the Fifth: I can neither entirely acquit Richard of it, nor condemn him; because there are no proofs on either side; and though a court of justice would, from that defect of evidence, absolve him; opinion may fluctuate backwards and forwards, and at last remain in suspense.

From Horace Walpole *Historic doubts on the Life and Reign of Richard III.*

The Character of this Prince has been in general very severely treated by Historians, but as he was a York, I am rather inclined to suppose him a very respectable Man. It has indeed been confidently asserted that he killed his two Nephews and his Wife, but it has also been declared that he did not kill his two Nephews, which I am inclined to believe true; and if this is the case, it may also be affirmed that he did not kill his Wife, for if Perkin Warbeck was really the Duke of York, why might not Lambert Simnel be the Widow of Richard. Whether innocent or guilty, he did not reign long in peace, for Henry Tudor E. of Richmond as great a villain as ever lived, made a great fuss about getting the Crown and having killed the King at the battle of Bosworth, he succeeded to it.

From Jane Austen.

Henry VII by Michael Sitium

THE TUDORS

Bust of Henry VII by Pietro
Torrigiano

Richard did indeed die on Bosworth Field, and the Hollow Crown was seized by Henry VII, the first Tudor, who made his claim in a fighting speech to his troops.

If ever God gave victory to men fighting in a just quarrel, no doubt, my fellows and friends, but He of his bountiful goodness will this day send us triumphant victory and a lucky journey over our proud enemy and arrogant adversary.

Our cause is so just, that no enterprise can be of more virtue both by the laws Divine and Civil; for, what can be a more honest, goodly, or godly quarrel, than to fight against a captain being an homicide and murderer of his own blood and progeny? – an extreme destroyer of his nobility, and to his and our country and the poor subjects of the same, a deadly mall, a fiery brand, and a burden untolerable?

He that calleth himself King, keepeth from me the crown and regiment of this noble realm and country, contrary to all justice and equity. Likewise, his mates and friends occupy your lands, cut down your woods, and destroy your manors, letting your wives and children range abroad for their living; which persons, for their penance and punishment, I doubt not but God, of His goodness, will either deliver into our hands as a great gain and booty, or cause them, being grieved and compuncted with the prick of their corrupt consciences, cowardly to fly and not abide the battle. Besides this, I assure you that there be yonder in that great battle men brought thither for fear and not for love, truly I doubt which is the greater, the malice of the soldiers toward their captain, or the fear of him conceived by his people. For surely this rule is infallible that, as ill men daily covet to destroy the good, so God appointeth the good to confound the ill.

Remember the victory is not gotten with the multitude of men, but with the courages of hearts and valiantness of minds. The smaller that our number is, the more glory is to us, if we vanquish. If we be overcome, yet no land is to be attributed to the victors, considering that ten men fought against one; and if we die, so glorious a death in so good a quarrel, neither fretting sorrow nor cancarding oblivion, shall be able to obfuscate or raze out of the book of fame either our names or our godly attempt.

And this one thing I assure you, that in so just and good a cause and so notable a quarrel, you shall find me this day rather a dead carrion on the cold ground, than a free

prisoner on a carpet in a lady's chamber. Let us, therefore, fight like invincible giants, and set on our enemies, like untimorous tigers, and banish all fear, like ramping lions. And now advance forward, true men against traitors, pitiful persons against murtherers, true inheritors against usurpers, the scourges of God against tyrants. Display my banner with a good courage; march forth like strong and robustious champions, and begin the battle like hardy conquerors. The battle is at hand, and the victory approacheth, and, if we shamefully recule or cowardly flee, we and all our sequel be destroyed and dishonoured for ever.

This is the day of gain, and this is the time of loss; get this day victory, and be conquerors; and lose this day's battle, and be villains; and, therefore, in the name of God and Saint George, let every man courageously advance forth his standard.

He was of an high mind, and loved his own will and his own way; as one that revered himself, and would reign indeed. Had he been a private man he would have been termed proud: but in a wise Prince, it was but keeping of distance; which indeed he did towards all; not admitting any near or full approach either to his power or to his secrets. For he was governed by none. His Queen (notwithstanding she had presented him with divers children; and with a crown also, though he would not acknowledge it) could do nothing with him. His mother he reverenced much, heard little.

To his confederates abroad he was constant and just; but not open. But rather such was his inquiry and such his closeness, as they stood in the light towards him, and he stood in the dark to them; yet without strangeness, but with a semblance of mutual communication of affairs.

He kept a strait hand on his nobility, and chose rather to advance clergymen and lawyers, which were more obsequious to him, but had less interest in the people; which made for his absoluteness, but not for his safety. Insomuch as I am persuaded it was one of the causes of his troublesome reign.

Neither did he care how cunning they were that he did employ: for he thought himself to have the master-reach. And as he chose well, so he held them up well. For it is a strange thing, that though he were a dark prince, and infinitely suspicious, and his times full of secret conspiracies and troubles; yet in twenty-four years reign he never put down or discomposed counsellor or near servant, save only

Stanley the Lord Chamberlain. As for the disposition of his
subjects in general towards him, it stood thus with him;
that of the three affections which naturally tie the hearts of
the subjects to their sovereign, – love, fear, and reverence, –
he had the last in height; the second in good measure; and
so little of the first, as he was beholding to the other two.

He was a Prince, sad, serious, and full of thoughts and
secret observations; and full of notes and memorials of his
own hand, especially touching persons; as whom to employ,
whom to reward, whom to inquire of, whom to beware of,
what were the dependencies, what were the factions, and
the like; keeping (as it were) a journal of his thoughts. There
is to this day a merry tale; that his monkey (set on as it was
thought by one of his chamber) tore his principal note-book
all to pieces; whereat the court which liked not those
pensive accounts was almost tickled with sport.

He was indeed full of apprehensions and suspicions, his
thoughts were so many, as they could not well always stand
together; but that which did good one way, did hurt
another. Neither did he at some times weigh them aright
in their proportions. Certainly that rumour which did him
so much mischief (that the Duke of York should be saved
and alive) was (at the first) of his own nourishing, because
he would have more reason not to reign in the right of
his wife.

For his pleasures, there is no news of them. And yet by
his instructions to Marsin and Stile touching the Queen of
Naples, it seemeth he could interrogate well touching
beauty. He did by pleasures as great as Princes do by
banquets, come and look a little upon them, and turn away.

No doubt, in him as in all men (and most of all in Kings)
his fortune wrought upon his nature, and his nature upon
his fortune. His times being rather prosperous than calm,
had raised his confidence by success, but almost marred his
nature by troubles. His wisdom, by often evading from
perils, was turned rather into a dexterity to deliver himself
from dangers when they pressed him, than into a providence
to prevent and remove them afar off. Whether it were the
shortness of his foresight, or the strength of his will, or the
dazzling of his suspicions, or what it was; certain it is that
the perpetual troubles of his fortunes (there being no more
matter out of which they grew) could not have been
without some great defects in his nature, customs, and
proceedings, which he had enough to do to save and
help with a thousand little industries and watches.

He was a comely personage, a little above just stature,
well and straight limbed, but slender. His countenance was

reverend, and a little like a churchman: and as it was not strange or dark, so neither was it winning or pleasing, but as the face of one well disposed. But it was to the disadvantage of the painter, for it was best when he spake.

From Francis Bacon *History of Henry VII.*

Henry, having achieved the throne, thought that a good European marriage would strengthen his position. Here are his instructions to his ambassadors concerning a proposed marriage to the Queen of Naples.

From instructions given by the King's highness to his servants, showing how they shall order themselves when they shall come to the presence of the old Queen of Naples and the young Queen her daughter.

At the coming to the said Queens we kneeled down before them and kissed their hands, and delivered my Lady Princess's letters unto them. First, the old Queen answered for herself as a noble, wise woman; and after the young Queen with a *sad* and a *noble* countenance, and with great *discretion*, uttered and spake such words as pleased her, not having *many words* but full steadfast, and with no high speech. The old Queen had the like words, and many more.

Item, specially to mark and note well the age and stature of the said young Queen, and the features of her body.

As to the age of the said young queen, it is seven and twenty years and not much more; and as to the stature of her person we cannot perfectly understand nor know, for commonly when that we came unto her presence her grace was sitting on a pillow.

    And as to the features of her body of the said young Queen, forasmuch as that at all times that we have seen her grace ever she had a great mantle of cloth on her in such wise after the manner of that country that a man shall not lightly perceive anything except only the visage, wherefore we could not be in certain of any such features of her body.

Item, specially to mark the favor of her visage, whether she be painted or not, and whether it be fat or lean, sharp or round, and whether her countenance be cheerful and amiable, frowning or melancholy, stedfast or light, or blushing in communication.

As far as that we can perceive or know, that the said Queen is not painted, and the favour of her visage is after her stature, of a very good compass, and amiable, and somewhat round and fat, and the countenance cheerful, not frowning, and steadfast, and not light nor bold-hardy in speech, but with a demure womanly shamefaced countenance, and of few words, as that we could perceive as we can think that she uttered the fewer words by cause that the Queen her mother was present, which had all the sayings.

Item, to note well her eyes, brows, teeth and lips.

The eyes of the said Queen be of colour brown, somewhat greyish; and her brows of a brown hair and very small, like a wire of hair; and her teeth fair and clean, and as far as we could perceive, well set; and her lips somewhat round and thick, according to the proportion of her visage, the which right well becometh the said Queen.

Item, to mark well the fashion of her nose, and the height and breadth of her forehead.

The fashion of her nose is a little rising in the midward, and a little coming or bowing towards the end, and she is much like nosed unto the Queen her mother.
     And as to her forehead, the height or the breadth thereof we could not perfectly discern, for the manner of the wearing of the kerchiefs or tuckers in that country is such that a man cannot well judge it, for their kerchowes coming down to their brows, and much the less we could come by the very knowledge of that cause for that the Queen weared black kerchiefs.

Item, to mark her arms, whether they be great or small, long or short.

As that we can perceive and know, that the arms of the said Queen be somewhat round and not very small.

Item, to mark her breasts and paps, whether they be big or small.

The said Queen's breasts be somewhat great and fully, and inasmuch as that they were trussed somewhat high, after the manner of the country, the which causeth her grace for to seem much the fullyer and her neck to be the shorter.

Item, to mark whether there appear any hair about her lips or not.

As far as that we can perceive and see, the said Queen hath no hair appearing about her lips nor mouth, but she is very clear skinned.

Item, that they endeavour them to speak with the said young Queen fasting, and to approach as near to her mouth as they honestly may, to the intent that they may feel the condition of her breath, whether it be sweet or not.

We could never come unto the speech of the said Queen fasting, wherefore we could nor might not attain to knowledge of that part of this article, notwithstanding at such other times as we have spoken and have had communication with the said Queen, we have approached as nigh unto her visage as that conveniently we might do, and we think verily by the favour of her visage and cleanness of her complexion and of her mouth that the said Queen is like for to be of a sweet savour and well aired.

Item, to inquire of the manner of her diet, and whether she be a great feeder or drinker, and whether she useth often to eat or drink, and whether she drinketh wine or water or both.

The said Queen is a good feeder, and eateth well her meat
twice on a day, and that her grace drinketh not often, and
that she drinketh most commonly water, and sometimes
that water is boiled with cinnamon, and sometimes she
drinketh ipocras, but not often.

*Item, the King's said servants shall also diligently inquire for
some cunning painter to the intent that the said painter may draw
a picture of the visage and semblance of the said young Queen as
like unto her as it can or may be conveniently done, which
picture and image they shall substantially note and mark in every
point and circumstance, so that it agree in similitude and likeness
as near as it may possible to the very visage, countenance, and
semblance of the said Queen.*

There was no answer made to this article and his majesty
did not marry the lady.

Portrait of Elizabeth of York

This Monarch soon after his accession married the Princess Elizabeth of York, by which alliance he plainly proved that he thought his own right inferior to hers, tho' he pretended to the contrary. By this Marriage he had two sons and two daughters, the elder of which Daughters was married to the King of Scotland and had the happiness of being grandmother to one of the first Characters in the World. But of her, I shall have occasion to speak more at large in future. The youngest, Mary, married first the King of France and secondly the D. of Suffolk, by whom she had one daughter, afterwards the Mother of Lady Jane Grey, who tho' inferior to her lovely Cousin the Queen of Scots, was yet an amiable young woman and famous for reading Greek while other people were hunting. It was in the reign of Henry the 7th that Perkin Warbeck and Lambert Simnel before mentioned made their appearance, the former of whom was set in the stocks, took shelter in Beaulieu Abbey, and was beheaded with the Earl of Warwick, and the latter was taken into the King's kitchen. His Majesty died and was succeeded by his son Henry whose only merit was his not being quite so bad as his daughter Elizabeth.

From Jane Austen.

Henry VIII started his reign auspiciously ; he had
everything on his side – he was well educated,
intelligent and, not least, handsome.

Henry VIII after Hans Holbein

His Majesty is the handsomest potentate I ever set eyes
upon; above the usual height, with an extremely fine calf to
his leg, his complexion very fair and bright, with auburn
hair combed straight and short, in the French fashion, and a
round face so very beautiful that it would become a pretty
woman, his throat being long and thick. He speaks French,
English and a little Italian, plays well on the lute and
harpsichord, sings from the book at sight, draws the bow
with greater strength than any man in England, and jousts
marvellously. Believe me, he is in every respect a most
accomplished prince.

From a letter from Piero Pasqualigo, Venetian Ambassador
Extraordinary, 1515.

Catherine of Aragon by
Johannes Corvus

Henry VIII needed a male heir. After eighteen years of marriage and only a daughter he decided to divorce Catherine of Aragon. At the trial she conducted her own defence.

'Catherine, Queen of England, come into the court.'

She could not come directly to the King for the distance which severed them, so she took pain to go about directly to the King, kneeling down at his feet in the sight of all the court and assembly to whom she said in effect in broken English, as followeth:

'Sir I beseech you for all the love that hath been between us, let me have justice and right, take of me some pity and compassion, for I am a poor woman, and a stranger, born out of your dominion. I have here no assured friend and much less indifferent counsel. I flee to you, as to the head of justice within this realm.

Alas, Sir, wherein have I offended you, or what occasion of displeasure have I designed against your will or displeasure? Intending (as I perceive) to put me from you, I take God and all the world to witness that I have ever been to you a true, humble, and obedient wife, ever comfortable to your will and pleasure that never said nor did anything to the contrary thereof, being always well pleased and contented with all things wherein you had any delight or dalliance, whether it were little or much. I never grudged in word or countenance, or showed a visage or spark of discontentation.

I loved all those whom ye loved, only for your sake, whether I had cause or no, and whether they were my friends or my enemies. This twenty years I have been your true wife or more, and by me ye have had divers children, although it hath pleased God to call them out of this world, which hath been no default in me.

And when ye had me at the first, I take God to be my judge, I was a true maid, without touch of man. And whether this be true or no, I put it to your conscience. If there be any just cause by the law that ye can allege against me, either of dishonesty or any other impediment to banish and put me from you, I am well content to depart, to my great shame and dishonour; and if there be none, then here I most lowly beseech you let me remain in my former estate, and receive justice at your princely hands.

Therefore I humbly require you to spare me the extremity

of this new court. And if ye will not, to God I commit my cause.'

'Madam, ye be called again.'

'It matters not. This is no indifferent court for me. I will not tarry.'

From Cavendish *Life of Cardinal Wolsey.*

— but having failed, when dying in her bed, made a last plea for their daughter, Mary, in a letter to the man she still thought of as her husband.

My Lord and Dear Husband:

I commend me unto you. The hour of my death draweth fast on, and my case being such, the tender love I owe you forceth me, with a few words, to put you in remembrance of the health and safeguard of your soul, which you ought to prefer before all worldly matters, and before the care and tendering of your own body, for the which you have cast me into many miseries and yourself into many cares. For my part I do pardon you all, yea, I do wish and devoutly pray God that He will also pardon you.

For the rest I commend unto you Mary, our daughter, beseeching you to be a good father unto her, as I heretofore desired. I entreat you also, on behalf of my maids, to give them marriage-portions, which is not much, they being but three. For all my other servants I solicit a year's pay more than their due, lest they should be unprovided for.

Lastly I do vow, that mine eyes desire you above all things.

NSINE SOLE
IRIS.

Henry's wooing of Anne Boleyn was long and hard. He wrote twice to Anne Boleyn:

Elizabeth, the 'Rainbow' portrait by Antonio Zuccaro

By revolving in my mind the contents of your last letters, I have put myself into great agony, not knowing how to interpret them – whether to my disadvantage (as I understand some of them) or not. I beseech you earnestly to let me know your real mind as to the love between us two. It is needful for me to obtain this answer, having been for a whole year wounded with the dart of love, and not yet assured whether I shall succeed in finding a place in your heart and affection.

This uncertainty has hindered me of late from declaring you my mistress, lest it should prove that you only entertain for me an ordinary regard. But if you please to do the duty of a true and loyal mistress, and give up yourself heart and body to me, who will be, as I have been, your most loyal servant (if your rigour does not forbid me), I promise you that not only the name shall be given you, but also that I will take you for my mistress, casting off all others that are in competition with you out of my thoughts and affections, and serving you only.

I beg you to give an entire answer to this my rude letter, that I may know on what and how far I may depend; but if it does not please you to answer me in writing, let me know some place where I may have it by word of mouth, and I will go thither with all my heart.

No more for fear of tiring you.

Written by the hand of him who would willingly remain Yours, H. Rex

Mine Own Sweetheart.

This shall be to advertise you of the great elengeness [loneliness] that I find here since your departing, for I assure you me thinketh the time longer now since your departing last than I was wont to do a whole fortnight. I think your kindness and my fervency of love causeth it; for, otherwise, I would not have thought it possible that for so little a while it should have grieved me.

But now that I am coming towards you, methinketh my pains be half removed; for also I am right well comforted in so much that my book maketh substantially for my matter, [the King's schemes for his divorce] in attending to which I have spent above four hours this day, which causes me now to write the shorter letter to you at this time, because of some pain in my head.

Wishing myself, especially an evening, in my sweetheart's arms, whose pretty duckies I trust shortly to kiss.
Written with the hand of him that was, is, and shall be
yours by his own will.

Anne Boleyn by Hans Holbein

But she too failed to provide a male heir, and after only
three years of marriage, she was charged with and
convicted of adultery, for which she was committed to the
Tower of London. She writes to Henry for her life:

Your Grace's displeasure and my imprisonment are things
so strange unto me, that what to write, or what to excuse,
I am altogether ignorant. To speak a truth, never a prince
had wife more loyal in all duty, and in all true affection,
than you have ever found in Anne Bulen – with which
name and place I could willingly have contented myself, if
God and Your Grace's pleasure had been so pleased. Neither
did I at any time so far forget myself in my exaltation or
received queenship, but that I always looked for such
alteration as I now find; for the ground of my preferment
being on no surer foundation than Your Grace's fancy, the
least alteration was fit and sufficient (I knew) to draw that
fancy to some other subject.

You have chosen me from a low estate to be your Queen
and companion, far beyond my desert or desire; if, then,
you found me worthy of such honour, Good your Grace,
let not any light fancy or bad counsel of my enemies
withdraw your princely favour from me; neither let that
stain – that unworthy stain – of a disloyal heart towards
your good grace ever cast so foul a blot on me, and on the
infant Princess your daughter.

Try me, good King, but let me have a lawful trial, and
let not my sworn enemies sit as my accusers and as my
judges; Yea, let me receive an open trial, for my truth shall
fear no open shames. But if you have already determined of
me, and that not only my death, but an infamous slander
must bring you the joying of your desired happiness, then I
desire of God that He will pardon your great sin herein,
and likewise my enemies, the instruments thereof; and
that He will not call you to a strait account for your
unprincely and cruel usage of me at His general judgment-
seat, where both you and myself must shortly appear; and
in whose judgment, I doubt not (whatsoever the world may
think of me), mine innocency shall be openly known and
sufficiently cleared.

Jane Seymour by Hans Holbein   Anne's brother, George, Viscount Rochford, may have
written this poem.

O Death, O Death rock her asleep
  Bring her to quiet rest,
Let pass her weary guiltless life
  Out of her careful breath.
Toll on thou passing bells,
  Ring out her doleful knell,
Let thy sound her death tell.
  Death doth draw nigh;
There is no remedy, for she must die.

After Jane Seymour's death Henry married Anne of Cleves
for political rather than dynastic reasons, but she
displeased him and was divorced and sent home. It was
his Chancellor Thomas Cromwell who lost his head over
this wife.

One of Henry's own poems, with its praise of constancy, rings strangely in this context.

As the holly groweth green,
  And never changeth hue,
So am I, and e'er have been,
  Unto my lady true.

  Green groweth the holly, so doth the ivy,
  Though wintry blasts blow ne'er so high,
  Green groweth the holly.

As the holly groweth green,
  With ivy all alone,
When flowers cannot be seen
  And greenwood leaves be gone,

  Green groweth the holly, so doth the ivy,
  Though wintry blasts blow ne'er so high,
  Green groweth the holly.

Now unto my lady
  Promise to her I make,
From all other only
  To her I me betake:

  Green groweth the holly, so doth the ivy,
  Though wintry blasts blow ne'er so high,
  Green groweth the holly.

Adieu, mine own lady,
  Adieu, my special,
Who hath my heart truly,
  Be sure, and ever shall.

  Green groweth the holly, so doth the ivy,
  Though wintry blasts blow ne'er so high,
  Green groweth the holly.

Catherine Howard by
Hans Holbein

It would be an affront to my Readers were I to suppose that they were not as well acquainted with the particulars of this King's reign as I am myself. It will therefore be saving them the task of reading again what they have read before, and myself the trouble of writing what I do not perfectly recollect, by giving only a slight sketch of the principal Events which marked his reign. Among these may be ranked Cardinal Wolsey's telling the father Abbott of Leicester Abbey that 'he was come to lay his bones among them,' the reformation in Religion and the King's riding through the streets of London with Anna Bullen. It is however but Justice, and my Duty to declare that this amiable Woman was entirely innocent of the Crimes with which she was accused, and of which her Beauty, her Elegance, and her Sprightliness were sufficient proofs, not to mention her solemn protestations of Innocence, the weakness of the Charges against her, and the King's Character; all of which add some confirmation, tho' perhaps but slight ones when in comparison with those before allegedly in her favour. Tho' I do not profess giving many dates, yet as I think it proper to give some and shall of course make choice of those which it is most necessary for the Reader to know, I think it right to inform him that her letter to the King was dated on the 6th of May. The Crimes and Cruelties of this Prince, were too numerous to be mentioned, (as this history I trust has fully shown;) and nothing can be said in his vindication, but that his abolishing Religious Houses and leaving them to the ruinous depredations of time has been of infinite use to the landscape of England in general, which probably was a principal motive for his doing it, since otherwise why should a Man who was of no Religion himself be at so much trouble to abolish one which had for ages been established in the Kingdom. His Majesty's 5th Wife was the Duke of Norfolk's Neice who, tho' universally acquitted of the crimes for which she was beheaded, has been by many people supposed to have led an abandoned life before her Marriage – of this however I have many doubts, since she was a relation of that noble Duke of Norfolk who was so warm in the Queen of Scotland's cause, and who at last fell a victim to it. The King's last wife contrived to survive him, but with difficulty effected it. He was succeeded by his only son Edward.

From Jane Austen.

ETATIS   SVÆ·21

KATHARINE PARRE

The fifth wife, Catherine Howard, seems to have been the not wholly innocent tool of her ambitious family, and she, like Anne Boleyn, paid for her adultery with her head. Catherine Parr, Henry's sixth wife, outlived him. She then wished to marry Thomas Seymour, the Protector's brother, but to do so she needed the permission of the new young king, ten-year-old Edward VI. He gave it willingly as he writes:

Catherine Parr by the Circle of Scrots

We thank you heartily, not only for the gentle acceptance of our suit moved unto you, but also for the loving accomplishing of the same, wherein you have declared not only a desire to gratify us, but also moved us to declare the goodwill likewise, that we bear to you in all your requests. Wherefore, ye shall not need to fear any grief to come or to suspect lack of aid in need, seeing that he, being mine uncle, is of so good a nature that he will not be troublesome by any means to you, and I of such mind that, for divers just causes, I must favour you. But even as without cause your merely require help against him whom you have put in trust with the carriage of these letters, so may I merely return the same request unto you, to provide that he may live with you also without grief, which have given him wholly unto you; and I will so provide for you both, that hereafter if any grief befall, I shall be a sufficient succour in your goodly and praiseworthy enterprises. Fare ye well, with much increase of honour and virtue in Christ.

Despite the view of a modern historian that "it is arguable that potentially Edward was the ablest of the Tudors" he excited a rather different view from another author:

There is no doubt that he was a most amiable little fellow, as docile as a lamb, if indeed his gentleness did not amount to absolute sheepishness. His flatterers say that he could speak five languages, and had a taste for music and physic, in the latter of which predilections we are quite unable to sympathise. As a quiet young gentleman at a preparatory school kept by ladies, Master Edward Tudor would have done credit no doubt to the establishment in which he might have been placed; but we would as soon select a sovereign from a seminary, at once, and take him from the bread-and-butter to the throne, as see the spirit of the

Edward VI by the
Circle of Scrots

monarchy diluted in milk-and-water, and the sceptre dwindling down into a king's patten spoon.

From Beckett's *Comic History of England*.

Edward VI was not strong and died aged sixteen, unmarried, in 1553.

As this prince was only nine years old at the time of his Father's death, he was considered by many people as too young to govern, and the late King happening to be of the same opinion, his mother's Brother the Duke of Somerset was chosen Protector of the realm during his minority. This Man was on the whole of a very amiable Character, and is somewhat of a favourite with me, tho' I would by no means pretend to affirm that he was equal to those first of Men Robert Earl of Essex, Delamere, or Gilpin. He was beheaded, of which he might with reason have been proud, had he known that such was the death of Mary Queen of Scotland; but as it was impossible that he should be conscious of what had never happened, it does not appear that he felt particularly delighted with the manner of it. After his decease the Duke of Northumberland had the care of the King and the Kingdom, and performed his trust of both so well that the King died and the Kingdom was left to his daughter in law the Lady Jane Grey, who has been already mentioned as reading Greek. Whether she really understood that language or whether such a study proceeded only from an excess of vanity for which I believe she was always rather remarkable, is uncertain. Whatever might be the cause, she preserved the same appearance of knowledge, and contempt of what was generally esteemed pleasure, during the whole of her life, for she declared herself displeased with being appointed Queen, and while conducting to the scaffold, she wrote a sentence in Latin and another in Greek on seeing the dead Body of her Husband accidentally passing that way.

From Jane Austen.

On Edward's death the Duke of Northumberland put his
own daughter-in-law (descended from Henry VII)
Lady Jane Grey on the throne. She was queen for nine
days only, by which time Mary had quelled
Northumberland's presumption.
Mary's tenure of the throne was not easy. Sir Thomas
Wyatt led a rebellion in part prompted by the news of
her alliance to Catholic Spain. Mary's speech in the
Guildhall won her great sympathy and is not unworthy of
her younger sister. She married Philip of Spain the
following year; it was not a success.

I am come unto you in mine own person to tell you that
which already you see and know; that is, how traitorously
and rebelliously a number of Kentishmen have assembled
themselves against us and you. Their pretence (as they said
at the first) was for a marriage determined for us, to the
which, and to all the articles thereof, ye have been made
privy. But since, we have caused certain of our privy
council to go again unto them, and to demand the cause of
this their rebellion; and it appeared then unto our said
council, that the matter of the marriage seemed to be but
a Spanish cloak to cover their pretended purpose against
our religion; for that they arrogantly and traitorously
demanded to have the governance of our person, the
keeping of the Tower, and the placing of our councillors.
Now, loving subjects, what I am ye right well know. I am
your Queen, to whom at my coronation, when I was
wedded to the realm and laws of the same (the spousal ring
whereof I have on my finger, which never hitherto was, nor
hereafter shall be left off) you promised your allegiance
and obedience unto me. And that I am the right and true
inheritor of the crown of this realm of England, I take all
Christendom to witness. My father, as ye all know,
possessed the same regal state, which now rightly is
descended unto me: and to him always ye showed yourselves most faithful and loving subjects; and therefore I
doubt not, but ye will show yourselves [such] likewise unto
me, and that ye will not suffer a vile traitor to have the
order and governance of our person, and to occupy our
estate, especially being so vile a traitor as Wyatt is.
    And I say to you on the word of a prince, I cannot tell
how naturally the mother loveth the child, for I was never
the mother of any, but certainly if a prince and governor
may as naturally and earnestly love her subjects, as the
mother doth love the child, then assure yourselves that I,

being your lady and mistress, do as earnestly love and favour you. And I, thus loving you, cannot but think that ye as heartily and faithfully love me; and then I doubt not but that we shall give these rebels a short and speedy overthrow.

As concerning the marriage, ye shall understand that I enterprised not the doing thereof without advice, and that by the advice of all our privy council. And as touching myself, I assure you, I am not so bent to my will, neither so precise nor affectionate, that either for mine own pleasure I would choose where I lust, or that I am so desirous, as needs I would have one. For God, I thank him, to whom be the praise therefore, I have hitherto lived a virgin, and doubt nothing, but with God's grace, I am able so to live still. But if, as my progenitors have done before me, it may please God, that I might leave some fruit of my body behind me, to be your governor, I trust you would not only rejoice thereat, but also I know it would be to your great comfort. And, certain, if I either did think or know, that this marriage were to the hurt of any of you my commons, or to the impeachment of any part or parcel of the royal state of this realm of England, I would never consent thereunto, neither would I ever marry while I lived. And on the word of a queen, I promise you, that if it shall not probably appear to all the nobility and commons, in the high court of parliament, that this marriage shall be for the high benefit and commodity of the whole realm, then will I abstain from marriage while I live.

And now good subjects, pluck up your hearts, and like true men, stand fast against these rebels, both our enemies and yours, and fear them not, for I assure you I fear them nothing at all.

Overleaf
Portrait of Mary I
Philip of Spain by Rubens
after Titian

ANNO DNI · 1544

ADI MARI · DOVGHTER TO
THE · MOST · VERTVOVS · PRIN
KINGE · HENRI · THE · EIGHT

THE · AGE · OF · XXVIII YERE

This woman had the good luck of being advanced to the throne of England, in spite of the superior pretensions, Merit and Beauty of her Cousins Mary Queen of Scotland and Jane Grey. Nor can I pity the Kingdom for the misfortunes they experienced during her Reign, since they fully deserved them, for having allowed her to succeed her Brother – which was a double piece of folly, since they might have foreseen that as she died without children, she would be succeeded by that disgrace to humanity, that pest of society, Elizabeth. Many were the people who fell martyrs to the protestant Religion during her reign; I suppose not fewer than a dozen. She married Philip King of Spain who in her sister's reign was famous for building Armadas. She died without issue, and then the dreadful moment came in which the destroyer of all comfort, the deceitful Betrayer of trust reposed in her, and the Murderess of her Cousin succeeded to the Throne.

From Jane Austen.

Mary died childless; she was succeeded by Anne
Boleyn's daughter, Elizabeth, aged twenty-five.

In an age of poets, she too tried her hand:

I grieve and dare not show my discontent,
I love and yet am forced to seem to hate,
I do, yet dare not say, I ever meant:
I seem stark mute, yet inwardly do prate.
   I am and am not, I freeze and yet am burn'd,
   Since from myself my other self I turn'd.

My care is like my shadow in the sun;
Follows one flying, flies when I pursue it,
Stands and lies by me, doth what I have done,
His too familiar care doth make me rue it.
   No means I find to rid him from my breast,
   Till by the end of things it be suppressed.

Some gentler passions slide into my mind,
For I am soft and made of melting snow.
Or be more cruel Love and so be kind,
Let me or float or sink, be high or low.
   Or let me live with some more sweet content,
   Or die and so forget what love ere meant.

Elizabeth's garden hat and
silk stockings and gloves

But her mastery of English prose, as well as her command over the loyalty of courtier and trooper alike, is evident from her great speech to the troops assembled at Tilbury before the Armada.

My loving people, we have been persuaded by some that are careful of our safety, to take heed how we commit ourselves to armed multitudes, for fear of treachery. But I assure you, I do not desire to live to distrust my faithful and loving people. Let tyrants fear. I have always so behaved myself that, under God, I have placed my chiefest strength and safeguard in the loyal hearts and goodwill of my subjects; and therefore I am come amongst you, as you see, at this time, not for my recreation and disport, but being resolved, in the midst and heat of battle, to live or die amongst you all, to lay down for my God, and for my kingdom, and for my people, my honour and my blood, even in the dust. I know I have the body of a weak and feeble woman, but I have the heart and stomach of a king, and of a king of England too, and I think foul scorn that Parma or Spain, or any prince of Europe should dare to invade the borders of my realm; to which, rather than any dishonour shall grow by me, I myself will take up arms, I myself will be your general, judge and rewarder of every one of your virtues in the field. I know, already for your forwardness you have deserved rewards and crowns; and we do assure you, in the word of a prince, they shall be duly paid you.

Foreigners were always impressed by her but never more so than at the end of her reign which lasted forty-five years.

Next came the Queen in the sixty-fifth year of her age, as we were told, very majestic; her face oblong, fair, but wrinkled; her eyes small yet black and pleasant; her nose a little hooked; her lips narrow; and her teeth black (a defect the English seem subject to from their too great use of sugar); she had in her ear two pearls, with very rich drops; she wore false hair and that red, her hands were small, her fingers long and her stature neither tall nor low; her air was stately; her manner of speaking mild and obliging.

From a letter by Paul Hentzen, tutor to a visiting nobleman.

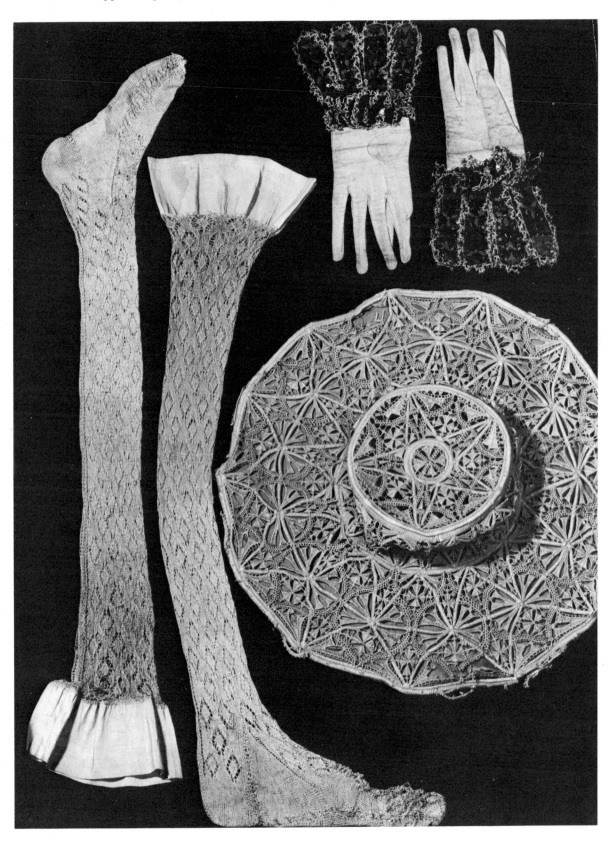

When I was fair and young and favour graced me,
Of many was I sought their mistress for to be.
But I did scorn them all and answered them therefore,
Go, go, go, seek some other where,
   Importune me no more.

How many weeping eyes I made to pine with woe,
How many sighing hearts I have no skill to show,
Yet I the prouder grew, and answered them therefore,
Go, go, go, seek some other where,
   Importune me no more.

Then spake fair Venus' son, that proud victorious boy,
And said, fine dame since that you been so coy,
I will so pluck your plumes that you shall say no more,
Go, go, go, seek some other where,
   Importune me no more.

When he had spake these words such change grew in my
                                              breast,
That neither day or night since that I could take any rest,
Then lo, I did repent of that I said before,
Go, go, go, seek some other where,
   Importune me no more.

Poem by Elizabeth.

What I learned of the Queen and the principal of her
Council before I had seen either her or any of them is that
when a man speaks to her, and especially when he says
something that is not pleasing, she interrupts not seldom;
and by reason of her interruptings she very often
misunderstands what is said to her and misrepresents it to
her Council. She is a haughty woman falling easily into
rebuke, and above all when any speak on behalf of the
King [of France].

In her own nature she is very avaricious, and when some
expense is necessary her Councillors must deceive her before
embarking her on it little by little. She thinks highly of
herself and has little regard for her servants and Council,
being of opinion that she is far wiser than they; she mocks
them and often cries out upon them. On their part, they,
even the Earl of Leicester, have given her a high opinion of
her wisdom and prudence. She thinks also that this is due to
her age, saying quite freely that she was intended for affairs
of state, even from her cradle, she told me so herself. She is
sixty years old.

She was strangely attired in a dress of silver cloth, white
and crimson, or silver 'gauze', as they call it. This dress had
slashed sleeves lined with red taffeta, and was girt about
with other little sleeves that hung down to the ground,
which she was for ever twisting and untwisting. She kept the
front of her dress open, and one could see the whole of her
bosom, and passing low, and often she would open the
front of this robe with her hands as if she was too hot. The
collar of the robe was very high, and the lining of the inner
part all adorned with little pendants of rubies and pearls,
very many, but quite small. She had also a chain of rubies
and pearls about her neck. On her head she wore a garland
of the same material and beneath it a great reddish-
coloured wig, with a great number of spangles of gold and
silver, and hanging down over her forehead some pearls,
but of no great worth. On either side of her ears hung two
great curls of hair, almost down to her shoulders and
within the collar of her robe, spangled as the top of her
head. Her bosom is somewhat wrinkled as well as [one can
see for] the collar that she wears round her neck, but lower
down her flesh is exceeding white and delicate, so far as one
could see.

As for her face, it is and appears to be very aged. It is long
and thin, and her teeth are very yellow and unequal,
compared with what they were formerly, so they say, and

Head of Elizabeth from her tomb in Westminster Abbey

on the left side less than on the right. Many of them are missing so that one cannot understand her easily when she speaks quickly. Her figure is fair and tall and graceful in whatever she does; so far as may be she keeps her dignity, yet humbly and graciously withal.

All the time she spoke she would often rise from her chair, and appear to be very impatient with what I was saying. She would complain that the fire was hurting her eyes, though there was a great screen before it and she six or seven feet away; yet did she give orders to have it extinguished, making them bring water to pour upon it. She told me that she was well pleased to stand up, and that she used to speak thus with the ambassadors who came to seek her, and used sometimes to tire them, of which they would on occasion complain. I begged her not to overtire herself in any way, and I rose when she did; and then she sat down again, and so did I.

From De Maisse *Journal.*

It was the peculiar misfortune of this Woman to have bad Ministers – Since wicked as she herself was, she could not have committed such extensive mischief, had not these vile and abandoned Men connived at, and encouraged her in her Crimes. I know that it has by many people been asserted and beleived that Lord Burleigh, Sir Francis Walsingham, and the rest of those who filled the cheif offices of State were deserving, experienced, and able Ministers. But oh! how blinded such writers and such Readers must be to true Merit, to Merit despised, neglected and defamed; if they can persist in such opinions when they reflect that these men, these boasted men were such scandals to their Country and their sex as to allow and assist their Queen in confining for the space of nineteen years, a Woman who if the claims of Relationship and Merit were of no avail, yet as a Queen and as one who condescended to place confidence in her, had every reason to expect assistance and protection; and at length in allowing Elizabeth to bring this amiable Woman to an untimely, unmerited, and scandalous Death.

From Jane Austen.

THE
STUARTS

The Stuarts:

James I slobbered at the mouth and had favourites; he was thus a Bad King.

With the ascension of Charles I to the throne we come at last to the Central Period of English History (not to be confused with the Middle Ages, of course) consisting in the *utterly memorable Struggle between the Cavaliers (Wrong but Wromantic) and the Roundheads (Right but Repulsive).*

Charles II was always very merry and was therefore not so much a king as a Monarch. During the civil war he had rendered valuable assistance to his father's side by hiding in all the oak-trees he could find. He was thus very romantic and popular and was able after the death of Cromwell to descend to the throne.

Although a Good Man, James II was a Bad King and behaved in such an irritating and arbitrary way that by the end of his reign the people had all gone mad. The final and irreparable madness of the people was brought on by James's action in bringing to trial Seven Bishops (Bancroft, Sancroft and Sacheveral others) for refusing to read Charles II's Declaration of Indulgence (which they thought would be dangerous under the circumstances), and when in addition it became known that James had confined his infant son and heir in a warming-pan the people lost control of themselves altogether and, lighting an enormous number of candles, declared that *the answer was an Orange.* James was thus compelled to abdicate.

William and Mary for some reason was known as The Orange in their own country of Holland, and were popular as King of England because the people naturally believed it was descended from Nell Glyn. Finally the Orange was killed by a mole while out riding and was succeeded by the memorable dead queen, Anne.

Queen Anne was considered rather a remarkable woman and hence was usually referred to as Great Anna, or Annus Mirabilis.

The queen had many favourites (all women), the most memorable of whom were Sarah Jenkins and Mrs Smashems, who were the first Wig and the first Tory. Sarah Jenkins was really the wife of the Duke of Marlborough, the famous General, inventor of the Ramillies Whig, of which Sarah wore the first example. Meanwhile the Whigs being the first to realize that the Queen had been dead all the time chose George I as King.

From *1066 and All That*.

James I of England and VI of Scotland was the son of
Mary Queen of Scots.

He was of middle stature, more corpulent through his
clothes than in his body, yet fat enough, his clothes ever
being made large and easy, the Doublets quilted for
stiletto proof, his Breeches in great pleats and full stuffed:
He was naturally of a timorous disposition, which was the
reason of his quilted Doublets: His eyes large, ever rolling
after any stranger came in his presence, insomuch, as many
for shame have left the room, as being out of countenance:
His Beard was very thin: His Tongue too large for his
mouth, which ever made him speak full in his mouth, and
made him drink very uncomely, as if eating his drink,
which came out into the cup of each side of his mouth. His
skin was as soft as Taffeta Sarsnet, which felt so, because he
never washed his hands, only rubbed his fingers' ends
slightly with the wet end of a Napkin: His Legs were very
weak, having had (as was thought) some foul play in his
youth, or rather before he was born, that he was not able to
stand at seven years of age, that weakness made him ever
leaning on other men's shoulders, his walk was ever
circular, his fingers ever in that walk fiddling about his
Codpiece: He was very temperate in his exercises, and in
his diet, and not intemperate in his drinking.
   He was very constant in all things (his Favourites excepted)
in which he loved change.
   He ever desired to prefer mean men in great places, that
when he turned them out again, they should have no friend
to bandy with them: And besides, they were so hated by
being raised from a mean estate, to over-top all men, that
every one held it a pretty recreation to have them often
turned out.
   There were living in this King's time, at one instant, two
Treasurers, three Secretaries, two Lord Keepers, two
Admirals, three Lord Chief Justices, yet but one in play,
therefore this King had a pretty faculty in putting out and
in: By this you may perceive in what his wisdom consisted,
but in great and weighty affairs even at his wit's end.
   Yet never cast down any (he once raised) from the height
of greatness, though from their wonted nearness, and
privacy; unless by their own default, by opposing his
change. In his Diet, Apparrel, and Journeys, he was very
constant; in his Apparrel so constant, as by his good will he
would never change his clothes until worn out to very rags:
His Fashion never: Insomuch as one bringing to him a Hat

of a Spanish Block, he cast it from him, swearing he neither loved them nor their fashions. Another time, bringing him Roses on his Shoes, he asked, if they would make him a ruffe-footed Dove? one yard of six penny Ribbon served that turn.

He naturally loved honest men, that were not over active, yet never loved any man heartily until he had bound him unto him by giving him some suite, which he thought bound the others love to him again; but that argued a poor disposition in him, to believe that anything but a Noble mind, seasoned with virtue, could make any firm love or union, for mercenary minds are carried away with a greater prize, but Noble minds, alienated with nothing but public disgraces.

He was very witty, and had as many ready witty jests as any man living, at which he would not smile himself, but deliver them in a grave and serious manner: He was very liberal, of what he had not in his own gripe, and would rather part with 100. li. he never had in his keeping, than one twenty shillings piece within his own custody. He spent much, and had much use of his Subjects purses, which bred some clashings with them in Parliament, yet would always come off, and end with a sweet and plausible close; and truly his bounty was not discommendable, for his raising Favourites was the worst.

By his frequenting Sermons he appeared Religious; yet his Tuesday Sermons (if you will believe his own Country-men, that lived in those times when they were erected, and well understood the cause of erecting them) were dedicated for a strange piece of devotion.

He was very crafty and cunning in petty things, as the circumventing any great man, the change of a Favourite, &c. insomuch as a very wise man was wont to say, he believed him the wisest fool in Christendom.

From Sir Anthony Weldon.

Masques and formal balls had been a great feature of
Queen Elizabeth's court. They continued into the new
reign although James found himself subjected to great
pressure from the rising group of Puritans.

A great feast was held, and after dinner the representation
of Solomon's Temple and the coming of the Queen of Sheba
was made, or (as I may better say) was meant to have been
made, before their Majesties.

The Lady who did play the Queen [of Sheba]'s part did
carry the most precious gifts to both their Majesties, but,
forgetting the steps arising to the canopy, overset her
caskets into his Danish Majesty's lap, and fell at his feet,
though I rather think it was in his face. Much was the hurry
and confusion; cloths and napkins were at hand, to make
all clean. His [Danish] Majesty then got up and would
dance with the Queen of Sheba but he knelt down and
humbled himself before her, and was carried to an inner
chamber and laid on a bed of state which was not a little
defiled with the presents of the Queen which had been
bestowed on his garments, such as wine, cream, jelly,
beverage, cakes, spices and other good matter. The
entertainment and show went forward, and most of the
presenters went backward, or fell down, wine did so occupy
their upper chambers. Now did appear, in rich dress, Hope,
Faith and Charity; Hope did essay to speak, but wine
rendered her endeavours so feeble that she withdrew, and
hoped the King would excuse her brevity; Faith was then
all alone, for I am certain she was not joined with good
works, and left the Court in a staggering condition;
Charity came to the King's feet, and seemed to cover the
multitude of sins her sisters had committed; in some sort
she made obeisance and brought gifts, but said she would
return home again as there was no gift which heaven had
not already given his Majesty. She then returned to Hope
and Faith, who were both sick and spewing in the lower
hall.

From Sir John Harington *Nugae Antiquae.*

James I anatomises a national abuse.

As every human body, dear countrymen, how wholesome soever, is notwithstanding subject to some sorts of diseases, so there is no Commonwealth or Body-Politic that lacks popular errors and corruptions. For remedy whereof, it is the King's to purge it of disease, by Medicines meet for the same.

Now surely in my opinion, there cannot be a more base and hurtful corruption than is the vile use of taking Tobacco in this Kingdom, which has moved me sharply to answer the abuses thereof.

Are you not guilty of sinful and shameful lust? that although you be troubled with no disease, but in perfect health, yet can you neither be merry at an Ordinary, nor Lascivious in the Stews, if you lack tobacco to provoke your appetite to any of those sorts of recreation, lusting after it as the children of Israel did in the wilderness after Quails?

Mollicies and delicacy were the wrack and overthrow, first of the Persian, and next the Roman Empire. Have you not reason then to be ashamed, and to forbear this filthy novelty, so basely grounded, so foolishly received, and so grossly mistaken in the right use thereof?

Now how you are by this custom disabled in your goods, let the gentry of this land bear witness, some of them bestowing three, some four hundred pounds a year upon this precious stink, which I am sure might be bestowed upon many far better uses.

And for the vanities committed in this filthy custom, is it not both great vanity and uncleanness, that at the table, a place of respect, of cleanliness, of modesty, men should not be ashamed, to sit tossing of tobacco pipes and puffing of the smoke of tobacco one to another, making the filthy smoke and stink thereof, to exhale athwart the dishes, and infect the air, when very often men that abhor it are at their repast? Surely smoke becomes a kitchen far better than a dining chamber, and yet it makes a kitchen also oftentimes in the inward parts of men, soiling and infecting them with an unctuous and oily kind of soot, as hath been found in some great tobacco takers, that after their death were opened. And not only meat time, but no other time nor action is exempted from the public use of this uncivil trick. And is it not a great vanity, that a man cannot heartily welcome his friend now, but straight they must be in hand with tobacco? No, it is become in place of a cure, a point of good fellowship, and he that will refuse to take a

pipe of tobacco among his fellows (though by his own election he would rather feel the savour of a sink) is accounted peevish and no good company, even as they do with tippling in the cold eastern countries. Yea, the mistress cannot in a more mannerly kind entertain her servant, than by giving him out of her fair hand a pipe of tobacco. But herein is not only a great vanity, but a great contempt of God's good gifts, that the sweetness of man's breath, being a good gift of God, should be wilfully corrupted by this stinking smoke.

Moreover, which is a great iniquity, and against all humanity, the husband shall not be ashamed to reduce thereby his delicate, wholesome, and clean complexioned wife to that extremity, that either she must also corrupt her sweet breath therewith, or else resolve to live in a perpetual stinking torment.

Have you not reason then to be ashamed, and to forbear this filthy novelty, so basely grounded, so foolishly received and so grossly mistaken in the right use thereof? In your abuse thereof sinning against God, harming yourselves both in persons and goods, and raking also thereby the marks and notes of vanity upon you; by the custom thereof making yourselves to be wondered at by all foreign civil nations, and by all strangers that come upon you to be scorned and contemned: a custom loathsome to the eye, hateful to the nose, harmful to the brain, dangerous to the lungs, and in the blackstinking fume thereof, nearest resembling the horrible Stygian smoke of the pit that is bottomless.

From James' Counterblaste to Tobacco.

Though this King had some faults, on the whole I cannot help liking him.

As I am myself partial to the roman catholic religion, it is with infinite regret that I am obliged to blame the Behaviour of any Member of it: yet Truth being I think very excusable in an Historian, I am necessitated to say that in this reign the roman catholics of England did not behave like Gentlemen to the protestants.

From Jane Austen.

Edward Hyde, Charles II's Chancellor at the Restoration,
was exiled by him and wrote in Holland, without
bitterness, one of the classics of English history, the
History of the Great Rebellion. Here he assesses Charles I.

But it will not be unnecessary to add the short character of his
person, that posterity may know the inestimable loss which
the nation then underwent, in being deprived of a prince
whose example would have had a greater influence upon
the manners and piety of the nation than the most strict
laws can have. To speak first of his private qualifications as
a man, before the mention of his princely and royal virtues:
he was, if ever any, the most worthy of the title of an honest
man – so great a lover of justice that no temptation could
dispose him to a wrongful action, except it were so disguised
to him that he believed it to be just. He had a tenderness
and compassion of nature which restrained him from ever
doing a hard-hearted thing. He was very punctual and
regular in his devotions, and was never known to enter
upon his recreations or sports – though never so early in the
morning – before he had been at public prayers; so that on
hunting-days his chaplains were bound to a very early
attendance. Though he was well pleased and delighted
with reading verses made upon any occasion, no man durst
bring before him anything that was profane or unclean;
that kind of wit never had any countenance then. He was so
great an example of conjugal affection that they who did
not imitate him in that particular did not brag of their
liberty.

His kingly virtues had some mixture and alloy that
hindered them from shining in full lustre, and from
producing those fruits they should have been attended with.
He was not in his nature bountiful, though he gave very
much; and he paused too long in giving which made those
to whom he gave less sensible of the benefit. He kept state
to the full, which made his court very orderly, no man
presuming to be seen in a place where he had no pretence
to be. He saw and observed men long before he received
any about his person, and did not love strangers, nor very
confident men. He was a patient hearer of causes, which he
frequently accustomed himself to, at the Council board. He
judged very well, and was dexterous in the mediating part;
so that he often put an end to causes by persuasion, which
the stubbornness of men's humours made dilatory in
courts of justice. He was very fearless in his person, but not
very enterprising. He had an excellent understanding but

was not very confident of it – which made him oftentimes change his own opinion for a worse, and follow the advice of a man that did not judge so well as himself. This made him more irresolute than the conjunction of his affairs would admit. If he had been of a rougher and more imperious nature, he would have found more respect and duty; and his not applying some severe cures to approaching evils proceeded from the lenity of his nature and the tenderness of his conscience, which in all cases of blood made him choose the softer way, and not hearken to severe counsels, how reasonably soever urged. He was always an immoderate lover of the Scottish nation, having not only been born there, but educated by that people.

After all this, when a man might reasonably believe that less than a universal defection of three nations could not have reduced a great king to so ugly a fate, it is most certain that in the very hour when he was thus wickedly murdered in the sight of the sun, he had as great a share in the hearts and affections of his subjects in general, was as much beloved, esteemed and longed-for by the people in general of three nations, as any of his predecessors had ever been.

Statue of Henrietta Maria by Herbert le Sueur

Civil war, provoked by Charles's arrest of the Five Members, broke out in 1642. Charles was arrested by the Commons in 1647, parleyed for a year and then induced the Scots to invade England on his behalf. This so angered Cromwell and many of his followers that they decided to try him. The trial took place in January 1649.

The King came into the Court, with his hat on; the Sergeant usher'd him in with the Mace. Colonel Hacker, and about thirty officers and gentlemen more, came as his Guard.

Mr. Cook, Solicitor General My Lord, in the behalf of the Commons of England, and of all the people thereof, I do accuse Charles Stuart, here present, of high treason, and high misdemeanours; and I do, in the name of the Commons of England, desire the charge may be read unto him.

The King Hold a little.

Lord President Sir, the Court commands the charge to be read; if you have any thing to say afterwards, you may be heard.

The charge read.

Whereas the Commons of England, assembled in Parliament have authorized us an high court of Justice for the trying and judging of Charles Stuart, as a tyrant, traitor, murderer, and public enemy of the Commonwealth, we do hereby charge him that he hath traitorously and maliciously levied war against the present Parliament and people, and that he hath thereby caused many thousands of the free people of this nation to be slain and many parts of the land spoiled, some of them even to desolation.

Lord President Sir, you have now heard your charge read . . . it is prayed to the Court, in the behalf of the Commons of England, that you answer to your charge.

I would know by what power I am called hither. I would know by what authority, I mean lawful – there are many unlawful authorities in the world, thieves and robbers by the high ways – but I would know by what authority I was brought from thence, and carried from place to place (and I know not what), and when I know what lawful authority, I shall answer. Remember I am your King, your lawful King, and what sins you bring upon your heads, and the judgment of God upon this land – think well upon it – I say, think well upon it, before you go further from one sin to a greater . . . In the mean time I shall not betray my trust; I have a trust committed to me by God, by old and lawful descent – I will not betray it to answer to a new unlawful authority; therefore resolve me that, and you shall hear of me.	The King
If you had been pleased to have observed what was hinted to you by the Court at your first coming hither, you would have known by what authority; which authority requires you in the name of the People of England, of which you are elected King, to answer them.	Lord President
No Sir, I deny that.	The King
If you acknowledge not the authority of the Court, they must proceed.	Lord President
England was never an elective kingdom, but an hereditary kingdom for near these thousand years; therefore let me know by what authority I am called hither. I do stand more for the liberty of my people than any here that come to my pretended judges.	The King
Sir, how really you have managed your trust is known; your way of answer is to interrogate the Court, which beseems not you in this condition. You have been told of it twice or thrice.	Lord President
I do not come here as submitting to the Court; I will stand as much for the privilege of the House of Commons, rightly understood, as any man here whatsoever. I see no House of Lords here that may constitute a parliament . . . Is this the bringing of the King to his Parliament? Is this the bringing an end to the treaty in the public faith of the world? Let me see a legal authority warranted by the Word of God, the Scriptures, or warranted by the constitutions of the kingdom, and I will answer.	The King

Lord President   Sir, you have propounded a question, and have been
answered. Seeing you will not answer, the Court will
consider how to proceed: in the mean time, those
that brought you hither are to take charge of you back
again . . .

Monday, Jan. 22, 1649

Lord President   Sir, you may remember at the last Court you heard a
charge read against you containing a charge of high treason
and other high crimes against this realm of England. You
heard likewise that you should give an answer to that
charge. You were then pleased to make some scruples
concerning the authority of this Court, and knew not by
what authority you were brought hither . . .

The King   When I was here last, 'tis very true I made that question,
and that a king cannot be tryed by any superior jurisdiction on earth; but it is not my case alone, it is the
freedom and the liberty of the People of England, and do
you pretend what you will, I stand more for their liberties.
For if power without law may make laws, may alter the
fundamental laws of the kingdom, I do not know what
subject he is in England that can be sure of his life or any
thing that he calls his own. Therefore when that I came
here, I did expect particular reasons to know by what law,
what authority you did proceed against me here . . .
   My reasons why in conscience and the duty I owe to God
first, and my People next, for the preservation of their
lives, liberties and estates – I conceive I cannot answer this
till I be satisfied of the legality of it . . .

Lord President   Sir, I must interrupt you, which I would not do, but that
what you do is not agreeable to the proceedings of any
Court of Justice: you are about to enter into argument, or
dispute concerning the authority of this Court and are
charged as an high delinquent.

The King   I do not know how a king can be a delinquent; but any
law that ever I heard of, all men – delinquents or what you
will – let me tell you they may put in demurrers against
any proceedings as legal, and I do demand that, and
demand to be heard with my reasons: if you deny that,
you deny reason.

You may not demur the jurisdiction of the Court: if you do, I must let you know that they overrule your demurrer. They sit here by the authority of the Commons of England, and all your predecessors and you are responsible to them.	Lord President
I deny that: shew me one precedent.	The King
Sir, you ought not to interrupt when the Court is speaking to you.	Lord President
I say, Sir, by your favour, that the Commons of England was never a Court of Judicature: I would know how they came to be so.	The King
Sir, you are not to be permitted to go on in that speech and these discourses.	Lord President

Then the Clerk of the Court read as followeth:

Charles Stuart, King of England, you have been accused on the behalf of the People of England of high treason and other crimes; the Court have determined that you ought to answer the same.	
I will answer the same so soon as I know by what authority you do this.	The King
If this be all that you will say, then gentlemen – you that brought the prisoner hither – take charge of him back again.	Lord President
I do require that I may give in my reasons why I do not answer, and give me time for that.	The King
Sir, 'tis not for prisoners to require.	Lord President
Prisoners? Sir, I am not an ordinary prisoner.	The King
The Court hath considered of their jurisdiction, and they have already affirmed their jurisdiction; if you will not answer, we shall give order to record your default.	Lord President
You never heard my reason yet.	The King
Sir, your reasons are not to be heard against the highest jurisdiction.	Lord President

The King   Shew me that jurisdiction where reason is not to be heard.

Lord President   Sir, we shew it you here – the Commons of England; and
                 the next time you are brought you will know more of the
                 pleasures of the Court – and, it may be, their final
                 determination.

The King   Shew me where ever the House of Commons was a Court
                 of Judicature of that kind.

Lord President   Sergeant, take away the prisoner.

The King   Well, Sir, remember that the King is not suffer'd to give
                 his reasons for the liberty and freedom of all his subjects.

Lord President   Sir, you are not to have liberty to use this language. How
                 great a friend you have been to the laws and liberties of the
                 people, let all England and the world judge.

The King   Sir, under favour it was the liberty, freedom, and laws of
                 the subject that ever I undertook, I defended my self with
                 arms, I never took up arms against the People, but for
                 the laws.

Lord President   The command of the Court must be obeyed. No answer
                 will be given to the charge.

The King   Well, Sir.

The Sentence

Whereas the Commons of England assembled in Parliament have authorised and constituted us an High Court of Justice for the trying and judging of Charles Stuart as a tyrant, traitor, murderer and public enemy of the Commonwealth; by virtue whereof the said Charles Stuart hath been three several times convented before this High Court.

That he, being King of England, out of a wicked design to erect and uphold in himself an unlimited and tyrannical power, hath traitorously and maliciously levied war against the present Parliament and people: and that he hath thereby procured many thousands of the free people of this nation to be slain, many families undone, and many parts of the land spoiled, some of them even to desolation; and that he thereby hath been and is the occasioner, author, and continuer of the said unnatural, cruel, and bloody wars, treasons, murders, rapines, burnings, spoils, desolations, damage, and mischief to this nation.

Now, therefore, upon serious and mature deliberation of the premises, this Court is fully satisfied in their judgments and consciences, that he is guilty of the wicked designs and endeavours in the said charge set forth.

For which this Court doth adjudge that he, the said Charles Stuart, as a tyrant, traitor, murderer, and public enemy to the good people of this nation, shall be put to death by the severing of his head from his body.

Charles I was executed at 2 pm on 30 January 1649 outside his palace at Whitehall.

This amiable Monarch seems born to have suffered misfortunes equal to those of his lovely Grandmother. Never certainly were there before so many detestable Characters at one time in England as in this period of its History; never were amiable men so scarce. The Events of this Monarch's reign are too numerous for my pen, and indeed the recital of any Events (except what I make myself) is uninteresting to me; my principal reason for undertaking the History of England being to prove the innocence of the Queen of Scotland, which I flatter myself with having effectually done, and to abuse Elizabeth, tho' I am rather fearful of having fallen short in the latter part of my scheme.

From Jane Austen.

Death warrant of Charles I

Charles II by Sir Peter Lely

For eleven years there was no crown, but after Cromwell's death it was apparent that the country wanted a monarch. On 29 May 1660 Charles II, who had been an exile in France, was restored.

He came with a triumph of over twenty thousand horse and foot brandishing their swords and shouting with inexpressible joy. The ways were strewn with flowers, the bells were ringing, the streets were hung with tapestry, and the fountains were running wine. The Mayor, Aldermen, and all the Companies, in their chains of gold, liveries, and banners, were present; also the lords and nobles. Everybody was clad in cloth of silver, gold and velvet; the windows and balconies were all set with ladies, trumpets and music, and myriads of people flocked the streets as far as Rochester, so that they took seven hours to pass through the city. I stood in the Strand and beheld it and blessed God. And all this was done without one drop of blood shed and by that very army that had rebelled against him.

From Evelyn *Diary.*

Charles II announced to Parliament his forthcoming marriage with Catherine of Braganza and married the lady in 1662.

My Lords and Gentlemen of the House of Commons: I will not spend the time in telling you why I called you hither; I am sure I am very glad to see you here.

I will tell you some news that I think will be very acceptable to you. I have been often put in mind by my friends that it was high time to marry. But there appeared difficulties enough in the choice, though many overtures have been made to me: and if I should never marry till I could make such a choice against which there could be no inconvenience, you would live to see me an old bachelor, which I think you do not desire to do. I can now tell you, not only that I am resolved to marry, but whom I resolve to marry: it is with the daughter of Portugal.

And I tell you with great satisfaction and comfort to myself that after many hours debate in my Privy Council, my Lords, without one dissenting voice (yet there were very few sat silent) advised me with all imaginable

cheerfulness to this marriage. Which I looked upon as very wonderful, and even as some instance of the approbation of God Himself; and so I make all the haste that I can to fetch you a Queen hither, who, I doubt not, will bring great blessings with her to you and me.

From a speech by Charles to the House of Commons.

But marriage did not induce fidelity, and Charles' instructions to Lord Clarendon to install his mistress, Lady Castlemaine, as one of his wife's ladies of the bedchamber followed fast upon his nuptials.

Portsmouth, May 21, 8 in the morning.

I arrived here yesterday about two in the afternoon, and as soon as I had shifted myself, I went to my wife's chamber, who I found in bed, by reason of a little cough, and some inclination to a fever, which was caused, as we physicians say, by having certain things stopped at sea which ought to have carried away those humours. But now all is in due course, and I believe she will find herself very well in the morning as soon as she wakes.

It was happy for the honour of the nation that I was not put to the consummation of the marriage last night; for I was so sleepy by having slept but two hours on my journey as I was afraid that matters would have gone very sleepily. I can now only give you an account of what I have seen a-bed; which, in short, is, her face is not so exact as to be called a beauty, though her eyes are excellent good, and not anything in her face that in the least degree can shock one. On the contrary, she has as much agreeableness in her looks altogether, as ever I saw; and if I have any skill in physiognomy, which I think I have, she must be as good a woman as ever was born. Her conversation, as much as I can perceive, is very good; for she has wit enough and a most agreeable voice. You would much wonder to see how well we are acquainted already. In a word, I think myself very happy; but am confident our two humours will agree very well together.

Overleaf
Marriage certificate of Charles II and Catherine of Braganza

Our Most Gra[cious]

Charles the Second, by the

Brittaine

And the most Illustrious Princess

Portugall, daughter to the deceased Don

present Don Alphonso, Kings of Portugall, were

the two & twentieth day of May, in the

yeare of his Majesties reigne, by the Right

Chappell Royall; in the presence of

...us **Soveraigne** ...Lord...

...race of God King of Great

...nce and Ireland Defender of the faith

...Dona Catarina Infanta of

...ountls and sister to ...

...ied at ...ortesmouth uppon thursd...

...of our Lord God 1662 beeing in the fourteenth

...Father In God Gilbert Lord Bishop of London ...as...

...the Nobilitie of his Ma.tie Dominions ...

...in 1662

Miniature of Catherine of
Braganza by Samuel Cooper

Hampton Court, Thursday evening

I forgot, when you were here last, to desire you to give
Brodericke good counsel not to meddle any more with
what concerns my Lady Castlemaine, and to let him have a
care how he is the author of any scandalous reports; for if I
find him guilty of any such thing, I will make him repent
of it to the last moment of his life.

And now I am entered on this matter, I think it necessary
to give you a little good counsel in it, lest you may think, by
making a further stir in the business, you may divert me
from my resolution, which all the world shall never do;
and I wish I may be unhappy in this world and in the world
to come if I fail in the least degree of what I have resolved,
which is of making my Lady Castlemaine of my wife's
bedchamber; and whosoever I find use any endeavours to
hinder this resolution of mine (except it be only to myself),
I will be his enemy to the last moment of his life.

You know how true a friend I have been to you. If you
will oblige me eternally, make this business as easy to me
as you can, of what opinion soever you are of, for I am resolved
to go through with this matter, let what will come of it,
which again I solemnly swear before Almighty God.

Therefore, if you desire to have the continuance of my
friendship, meddle no more with this business, except it be
to bear down all false and scandalous reports, and to
facilitate what I am sure my honour is so much concerned
in. And whosoever I find to be my Lady Castlemaine's
enemy in this matter, I do promise, upon my word, to be
his enemy as long as I live.

Two letters by Charles to Clarendon.

I pass all my hours in a shady old grove,
But I live not the day when I see not my love:
I survey every walk now my Phyllis is gone,
And sigh when I think we were there all alone.
　　Oh then 'tis I think there's no hell
　　Like loving too well.

But each shade and each conscious bow'r when I find,
Where I once have been happy, and she has been kind,
When I see the print left of her shape on the green,
I imagine the pleasure may yet come again.
　　O then 'tis I think no joys are above
　　The pleasures of love.

While alone to myself I repeat all her charms,
She I love may be lock'd in another man's arms;
She may laugh at my cares, and so false she may be,
To say all the kind thoughts she before said to me.
　　O then 'tis O then, that I think there's no hell
　　Like loving too well.

But when I consider the truth of her heart,
Such an innocent passion, so kind without art;
I fear I have wrong'd her, yet hope she may be
So full of true love to be jealous of me.
　　O then 'tis I think that no joys are above
　　The pleasures of love.

Poem by Charles.

Those who knew his Face, fixed their Eyes there; and thought it of more Importance to see, than to hear what he said. His Face was as little a Blab as most Mens, yet though it could not be called a prattling Face, it would sometimes tell Tales to a good Observer.

It may be said that his Inclinations to Love were the Effects of Health, and a good Constitution, with as little mixture of the Seraphick part as ever Man had: And though from that Foundation Men often raise their Passions; I am apt to think his stayed as much as any Man's ever did in the lower Region. This made him like easy Mistresses: They were generally resigned to him while he was abroad, with an implied Bargain.

After he was restored, Mistresses were recommended to him; which is no small matter in a Court, and not unworthy the Thoughts even of a Party. A Mistress either dexterous in herself, or well-instructed by those that are so, may be very useful to her Friends, not only in the immediate Hours of her Ministry, but by her Influences and Insinuations at other times. It was resolved generally by others, whom he should have in his Arms, as well as whom he should have in his Councils. Of a Man who was so capable of choosing, he chose as seldom as any Man that every [sic] lived.

He had more property, at least in the beginning of his Time, a good Stomach to his Mistresses, than any great Passion for them. His taking them from others was never learnt in a Romance; and indeed fitter for a Philosopher than a Knight-Errant. His Patience for their Frailties shewed him no exact Lover.

His Wit consisted chiefly in the Quickness of his Apprehension. His Apprehension made him find Faults, and that led him to short Sayings upon them, not always equal, but often very good.

By his being abroad, he contracted a Habit of conversing familiarly, which added to his natural Genius, made him very apt to talk; perhaps more than a very nice judgment would approve.

His Wit was better suited to his Condition before he was restored than afterwards. The Wit of a Gentleman, and that of a crowned Head, ought to be different things. As there is a Crown Law, there is a Crown Wit too. To use it with Reserve is very good, and very rare. There is a Dignity in doing things seldom, even without any other Circumstance. Where Wit will run continually, the Spring is apt to fail; so that it groweth vulgar, and the more it is practised, the more it is debased.

He was so good at finding out other Mens weak Sides, that it made him less intent to cure his own: That generally happeneth.

He grew by Age into a pretty exact Distribution of his Hours, both for his Business, Pleasures, and the Exercise for his Health, of which he took as much care as could possibly consist with some Liberties he was resolved to indulge in himself. He walked by his Watch, and when he pulled it out to look upon it, skilful Men would make haste with what they had to say to him.

He could not properly be said to be either covetous or
liberal; his desire to get was not with an Intention to be
rich; and his spending was rather an Easiness in letting
Money go, than any premeditated Thought for the
Distribution of it. He would do as much to throw off the
burden of a present Importunity, as he would to relieve
a want.

When once the Aversion to bear Uneasiness taketh place
in a Man's Mind, it doth so check all the Passions, that they
are dampt into a kind of Indifference; they grow faint and
languishing, and come to be subordinate to that fundamental
Maxim of not purchasing any thing at the price of a
Difficulty. This made that he had as little Eagerness to
oblige, as he had to hurt Men; the Motive of his giving
Bounties was rather to make Men less uneasy to him, than
more easy to themselves; and yet no ill-nature all this while.

The truth is, the calling of a King, with all its glittering,
hath such a weight upon it, that they may rather expect to
be lamented than envied. Let his Royal Ashes then lie soft
upon him. If all who are akin to his Vices should mourn for
him, never Prince would go better attended to his grave.

From the Marquess of Halifax.

James II with Anne Hyde,
Mary and Anne by Sir Peter
Lely

James II, who as Duke of York had been exiled to France by his brother Charles II to avoid trouble on account of his Catholicism, returned, as legitimate heir, to the throne.

Upon this I will digress a little, to give an account of the Duke's character, whom I knew for some years so particularly, that I can say much upon my own knowledge. He was very brave in his youth, and so much magnified by monsieur Turenne, that, till his marriage lessened him, he really clouded the King, and passed for the superior genius. He was naturally candid and sincere, and a firm friend, till affairs and his religion wore out all his first principles and inclinations. He had a great desire to understand affairs: and in order to that he kept a constant journal of all that passed, of which he shewed me a great deal. The Duke of Buckingham gave me once a short but severe character of the two brothers: It was the more severe, because it was true: the King (he said) could see things if he would, and the Duke would see things if he could. He had no true judgment, and was soon determined by those whom he trusted: but he was obstinate against all other advices. He was bred with high notions of the kingly authority, and laid it down for a maxim, that all who opposed the King were rebels in their hearts. He was perpetually in one amour or other, without being very nice in his choice: upon which the King said once, he believed his brother had his mistresses given him by his priests for penance.

He was naturally eager and revengeful: and was against the taking off any that set up in an opposition to the measures of the court, and who by that means grew popular in the House of Commons. He was for rougher methods. He continued for many years dissembling his religion, and seemed zealous for the church of England: but it was chiefly on design to hinder all propositions that tended to unite us among ourselves.

From Bishop Burnet *History of his Own Time.*

Mary of Modena by
William Wissing

Though a libertine, James was diligent, methodical and fond of authority and business. His understanding was singularly slow and narrow, and his temper obstinate, harsh, and unforgiving. That such a prince should have looked with no good will on the free institutions of England, and on the party which was peculiarly zealous for those institutions, can excite no surprise.

In the mind of James there was a great conflict. We should do him injustice if we supposed that a state of vassalage was agreeable to his temper. He loved authority and business. He had a high sense of his personal dignity. Nay he was not altogether destitute of a sentiment which bore some affinity to patriotism. It galled his soul to think that the kingdom which he ruled was of far less account in the world than many states which possessed smaller natural advantages; and he listened eagerly to foreign ministers when they urged him to assert the dignity of his rank, to place himself at the head of a confederacy, to become the protector of injured nations, and to tame the pride of that power which held the continent in awe. Such exhortations made his heart swell with emotions unknown to his careless and effeminate brother.

His second wish was to be feared and respected abroad. But his first wish was to be absolute master at home. Between the incompatible objects on which his heart was set, he, for a time went irresolutely to and fro. The struggle in his own breast gave to his public acts a strange appearance of indecision and insincerity.

The obstinate and imperious nature of the King gave great advantages to those who advised him to be firm, to yield nothing, and to make himself feared. One state maxim had taken possession of his small understanding, and was not to be dislodged by reason. To reason, indeed, he was not in the habit of attending. His mode of arguing, if it is to be so called, was one not uncommon among dull and stubborn persons who are accustomed to be surrounded by their inferiors. He asserted a proposition; and, as often as wiser people ventured respectfully to show that it was erroneous, he asserted it again, in exactly the same words, and conceived that, by doing so, he at once disposed of all objections. 'I will make no concessions', he often repeated; 'my father made concessions, and he was beheaded.'

From Macaulay *History of England from the Reign of James II.*

James had first married Anne Hyde, daughter of the Earl of Clarendon, by whom he had two daughters Mary and Anne, both of whom succeeded to the throne. On Anne Hyde's death he had married Mary of Modena and a son was born of this marriage under somewhat suspicious circumstances as Mary and Anne relate on page 208. James II's intractability over his religion forced him to send his wife and baby out of England, and he followed them himself later.

Things being come to that extremity I have been forced to send away the Queen and my son the Prince of Wales that they might not fall into the enemy's hands, which they must have done had they stayed, I am obliged to do the same thing, and endeavour to secure myself the best I can, in hopes it will please God, out of His infinite mercy to this unhappy nation, to touch their hearts with true loyalty and honour. If I could have relied upon all my troops I might not have been put to this extremity I am in, and could at least have had one blow for it; but thought I know there are many loyal and brave men amongst you, yet you know yourself, and several of the general officers told me, I was in no ways advisable to venture myself at their head. There remains nothing more for me but to thank you and all those officers and soldiers who have stuck to me and been truly loyal.

From a letter from James to one of his generals.

The Glorious Revolution put William and Mary on the
throne as joint rulers.

I saw the new Queen and King proclaimed the very
next day after her coming to Whitehall, Wednesday,
13th February, with great acclamation and general good
reception. Bonfires, bells, guns, &c. It was believed that
both, especially the Princess, would have showed some
(seeming) reluctance at least, of assuming her father's
Crown, and made some apology, testifying by her regret
that he should by his mismanagement necessitate the Nation
to so extraordinary a proceeding, which would have
showed very handsomely to the world, and according to
the character given of her piety; consonant also to her
husband's first declaration, that there was no intention of
deposing the King but of succouring the Nation; but
nothing of all this appeared; she came into Whitehall
laughing and jolly, as to a wedding, so as to seem quite
transported. She rose early the next morning, and in her
undress, as it was reported, before her women were up,
went about from room to room to see the convenience of
Whitehall; lay in the same bed and apartment where the
late Queen lay and within a night or two sat down to play
at basset, as the Queen her predecessor used to do. She
smiled upon and talked to everybody, so that no change
seemed to have taken place at Court since her last going
away. This carriage was censured by many. She seems to be
of a good nature, and that she takes nothing to heart:
whilst the Prince her husband has a thoughtful countenance,
is wonderfully serious and silent, and seems to treat all
persons alike gravely, and to be very intent on affairs:
Holland, Ireland, and France calling for his care.

From Evelyn *Diary*

The Prince had been much neglected in his education; for all his life long he hated constraint. He spoke little. He put on some appearance of application: but he hated business of all sorts. Yet he hated talking, and all house games, more. This put him on a perpetual course of hunting, to which he seemed to give himself up, beyond any man I ever knew: but I looked on that always, as a flying from company and business. The depression of France was the governing passion of his whole life. He had not vice, but of one sort, in which he was very secret. He had a way that was very affable and obliging to the Dutch. But he could not bring himself to comply enough with the temper of the English, his coldness and slowness being very contrary to the genius of the nation.

William III by William Wissing

The Princess possessed all that conversed with her with admiration. Her person was majestic, and created respect. She had great knowledge, with a true understanding, and a noble expression. There was a sweetness in her deportment that charmed, and an exactness in piety and of virtue that made her a pattern to all that saw her. The King gave her no appointments to support the dignity of a king's daughter. Nor did he send her any presents of jewels, which was thought a very indecent, and certainly a very ill advised thing. For the settling an allowance for her and the Prince would have given such a jealousy of them, that the English would have apprehended a secret correspondence and confidence between them: and the not doing it shewed the contrary very evidently. But, though the Prince did not increase her court, and state upon this additional dignity, she managed her privy purse so well, that she became eminent in her charities: and the good grace with which she bestowed favours did always increase their value. She had read much, both in history and divinity. And when a course of humours in her eyes forced her from that she set herself to work with such a constant diligence, that she made the ladies about her ashamed to be idle. She knew little of our affairs, till I was admitted to wait on her. And I began to lay before her the state of our court, and the intrigues in it ever since the restoration: which she received with great satisfaction, and shewed true judgment, and a good mind, in all the reflections that she made.

From Bishop Burnet *History of The Reign of King James the Second.*

Mary by William Wissing

Mary's marriage to William of Orange ensured that England and Holland should unite to fight the territorial aggression of France under Louis XIV. Count Tallard, who was to be beaten by Marlborough at Blenheim, spent some time in London as Louis' ambassador. Neither he nor his master cared for William.

London, May 9, 1698

The King of England is very far from being master here; he is generally hated by all the great men and the whole of the nobility: I could not venture to say despised, for in truth that word cannot be applied to him, but it is the feeling which all those whom I have just mentioned entertain towards him. It is not the same with the people, who are very favourably inclined towards him, yet less so than at the beginning. The friendship which this Prince shows to the Dutch, the intimacy in which he lives with them and with foreigners and the declared favour of the Earl of Albemarle, who is a very young man, have produced the effect which I have mentioned.

No Englishman has any real share in public affairs, except the Lord Chancellor, a man of about thirty-seven or thirty-eight years of age, whom the King has placed in that office, much attached to that Prince – very honest, and much esteemed by all parties. He is, however, employed solely on the home affairs of the kingdom.

The King is accused of being idle, at least of not being so laborious as he should be. He dines or sups three times a week with the Earl of Albemarle, and a short time before setting out for Newmarket he one day sat five hours at table.

King James has still friends in this country; and it is true that the present King has no solid foundation for the strengthening of his power in this country, except his army, of which he is the master, and the vicinity of the Dutch, who are also at his disposal. He has given the whole weight of Parliament to the House of Commons; the House of Lords has no credit whatever.

The journey which the King intends to make to Holland gives so much uneasiness to this nation, that it is much questioned if he will undertake it, at least such is the report; but perhaps it is only on account of Parliament. So much is certain that the situation of the King is still very precarious, and that the moment which has given repose to all the world, has been but the beginning of troubles to this prince.

From a letter by Count Tallard to Louis XIV.

N MARY.   WISSING

The birth of a half-brother to Mary and Anne – who became known to history as the Old Pretender – was of such consequence to the issue of the succession that it was not surprising that Mary, then in Holland, should evince such interest in his birth and question her sister Anne in London so closely about the event itself.

Whether the Queen [Mary of Modena] *desired at any time any of the ladies, in particular the Princess of Denmark* [Anne], *to feel her belly, since she thought herself quick, or of late.*

I never heard anybody say they felt the child stir; but I am told Lady Sunderland and Mme Mazarin say they felt it at the beginning. Mrs Dawson tells me she has seen it stir, but never felt it.

Whether the milk, that, as is said, was in the Queen's breasts, was seen by many, or conducted in a mystery?

I never saw any milk; but Mrs Dawson says she has seen it upon her smock and that it began to run at the same time as it used to do of her other children.

Whether the astringents that the Queen is said to have taken, were taken by her openly, or if a mystery was made of that? What doctors were consulted about the Queen before and since her being at the Bath?

For what they call restringing draughts, I saw her drink two of them; and I don't doubt she drank them frequently and publicly before her going to the Bath.

Whether the treating of the Queen's breasts for drawing back the milk, and the giving her clean linen has been managed openly or mysteriously?

All I can say to this article is that once in the discourse Mrs Bromley told Mrs Roberts, one day Mrs Roger's [Lady Sunderland's] daughter – came into the room when Mrs Mansell [the Queen] was putting off her clouts, and she was very angry at it, because she did not care to be seen when she was shifting.

At what hour did the Queen's labour begin?

She fell in labour about eight o'clock (a.m.)

At what hour was the notice of it sent to the King?

She sent for the King at that time, who had been up a
quarter of an hour, having lain with her that night, and was
then dressing.

*At what time came the King with the Council into the Queen's
chamber?*

They came into the room present after the Queen-Dowager
came, which is about half an hour before she was brought
to bed.

*Whether did any woman, besides the confidants, see the Queen's
face when she was in labour? And, whether she had the looks of a
woman in labour? Who was in the room, both men and women?*

The foot curtains of the bed were drawn, and the two sides
were open. When she was in great pain, the King called in
haste for my Lord Chancellor, who came up to the bedside
to show he was there; upon which the rest of the Privy
Councillors did the same thing. Then the Queen desired
the King to hide her face with his head and periwig, which
he did, for she said she could not be brought to bed and
have so many men look upon her; for all the Council stood
close at the bed's feet, and Lord Chancellor upon the step.

Who took the child when it was born?

As soon as the child was born the midwife cut the navel-
string, because the after-burthen did not follow quickly;
and then she gave it to Mrs Labadie who, as she was going
by the bedside, cross the step, to carry it into the little
chamber, the King stopped her and said to the Privy
Councillors that they were witnesses there was a child born,
and bid them follow it into the next room and see what it
was, which they all did; for till after they came out again, it
was not declared what it was; but the midwife had only
given a sign that it was a son, which is what had been done
before.

*Whether in any former labour the Queen was delivered so
mysteriously, so suddenly, and so few being called for?*

Her labour never used to be so long.

If many observed the child's limbs being slender at first, and their appearing all of a sudden to be round and full? Who is about it, rockers and dry-nurse? If everybody is permitted to see the child at all hours, dressed and undressed?

I never heard what you say of the child's limbs. As for seeing it dressed or undressed, they avoid it as much as they can. By all I have seen and heard, sometimes they refuse almost everybody to see it; and that is, when they say it is not well; and methinks there is always a mystery in it, for one does not know whether it be really sick and they fear one should know it, whether it is well, and they should have one think it is sick, as the other children used to be. In short, it is not very clear anything they do; and for the servants, from the highest to the lowest, they are all papists.

Anne was married to Prince George of Denmark, of whom Charles II had said 'I have tried him drunk and I have tried him sober and there is nothing in him'. She herself was mean and stupid and life at court was dull beyond compare. The best known quoted tag about her is 'Queen Anne is dead'.

There was a drawing room today at Court but so few company that the Queen sent for us into her bedchamber, where we made our bows, and stood about twenty of us round the room while she looked at us round with a fan in her mouth and once a minute said about three words to some that were nearest her; and then she was told dinner was ready, and went out.

From Jonathan Swift *Journal to Stella.*

Anne by J. Closterman

George of Denmark by John Riley

Anne was dominated by the more powerful personality of Sarah, Duchess of Marlborough, who used her friendship with the Queen to further her husband's career and fortune. In 1702 Anne (Morley) was only too anxious to help her friend Sarah (Mrs Freeman) but by 1709 they had fallen out. (Amy Rainsford was a starcher and seamstress to Anne for many years.)

St James's, December 16, 1702.

I cannot be satisfied with myself without doing something towards making up what has been so maliciously hindered in the Parliament, and therefore I desire my dear Mrs Freeman and Mr Freeman would be so kind as to accept of two thousand a year out of the privy purse, besides the grant of the five. This can draw no envy, for nobody need know. Not that I would disown what I give to people that deserve, especially where it is impossible to reward the deserts, but you may keep it a secret or not, as you please. I beg my dear Mrs Freeman would never any way give me an answer to this, only comply with the desires of your poor unfortunate, faithful Morley, that loves you most tenderly and is with the sincerest passion imaginable yours.

Windsor, October, 1709.

I had writ so long a letter to you yesterday, which I desired Lord Treasurer to send, when I received yours, that I could not then write more, or I should not have been so long answering it. You need not have been in such haste, for Rainsford is pretty well again, and I hope will live a great while. If she should die, I will then turn my thoughts to consider who I know that I would like in that place, that being a post that next my bedchamber woman is the nearest to my person of any of my servants; and I believe nobody – nay, even yourself, if you would judge impartially – could think it unreasonable that I should take one in a place so near my person that were agreeable to me.

   I know this place is reckoned under your office, but there is no office whatsoever that has the entire disposal of anything under them, but I may put in any one I please when I have a mind to it.

Two letters from Anne to Sarah, Duchess of Marlborough.

A man of twenty at the Restoration would have been
seventy-four at the time of George I's accession.

In good King Charles' golden days
When loyalty no harm meant,
A zealous High Churchman was I
And so I got preferment.
To teach my flock I never missed,
Kings are by God appointed
And damned are those that dare resist,
Or touch the Lord's anointed.
    And this is the law that I'll maintain
    Until my dying day, sir,
    That whatsoever King may reign
    I'll be the vicar of Bray, sir.

When royal James obtained the crown
And Popery came in fashion,
The penal laws I hooted down,
And read the Declaration.
The Church of Rome I found would fit
Full well my constitution
And had become a Jesuit,
But for the revolution.
    And this is the law that I'll maintain
    Until my dying day, sir,
    That whatsoever King may reign
    I'll be the vicar of Bray, sir.

When William was our King declared,
To air our nation's grievance,
With this new wind about I steered
And swore to him allegiance.
Old principles I did revoke,
Set conscience at a distance;
For passive obedience was a joke,
A jest was non-resistance.
    And this is the law that I'll maintain
    Until my dying day, sir,
    That whatsoever King may reign
    I'll be the vicar of Bray, sir.

When gracious Anne became our queen
The Church of England's glory,
Another face of things was seen
And I became a Tory.
Occasional Conformists base,
I damned their moderation;
And thought the church in danger was
By such prevarication.
   And this is the law that I'll maintain
   Until my dying day, sir,
   That whatsoever King may reign
   I'll be the vicar of Bray, sir.

When George in pudding-time came o'er
And moderate men looked big, sir,
I turned a cat-in-pan once more
And so became a Whig, sir.
And thus preferment I procured
From our new Faith's Defender,
And almost every day abjured
The Pope and the Pretender.
   And this is the law that I'll maintain
   Until my dying day, sir,
   That whatsoever King may reign
   I'll be the vicar of Bray, sir.

The Illustrious House of Hanover
And Protestant Succession,
To these I do allegiance swear
While they can keep possession,
For in my faith and loyalty
I never more will falter
And George my lawful King shall be . . .
Until the times do alter.
   And this is the law that I'll maintain
   Until my dying day, sir,
   That whatsoever King shall reign
   I'll be the vicar of Bray, sir.

THE HANOVERIANS

George I by D. Stevens (?)

George was fifty-four when he acceded to the throne; he spoke little English and when he arrived London was shrouded in thick fog.

George had been married to Sophia Dorothea of Celle, but had imprisoned her for alleged adultery shortly after their marriage. He had divorced her in 1694 and she spent the remaining thirty-two years of life in prison at Ahlden.

In 1700, the little Duke of Gloucester, the last of poor Queen Anne's children, died, and the folks of Hanover straightway became of prodigious importance in England. The Electress Sophia was declared the next in succession to the English throne. George Louis was Duke of Cambridge; grand deputations were sent over from our country to Deutschland; but Queen Anne, whose weak heart hankered after her relatives at St Germains, never could be got to allow her cousin, the Elector Duke of Cambridge, to come and pay his respects to her Majesty, and take his seat in her House of Peers. Had the Queen lasted a month longer; had the English Tories been as bold and resolute as they were clever and crafty; had the Prince whom the nation loved and pitied been equal to his fortune, George Louis had never talked German in St James's Chapel Royal.

When the crown did come to George Louis he was in no hurry about putting it on. He waited at home for a while; took an affecting farewell of his dear Hanover and Herrenhausen; and set out in the most leisurely manner to ascend 'the throne of his ancestors,' as he called it in his first speech to Parliament. He brought with him a compact body of Germans, whose society he loved, and whom he kept around the royal person. He had his faithful German chamberlains; his German secretaries; his negroes, captives of his bow and spear in Turkish wars; his two ugly, elderly German favourites, Mesdames of Kielmansegge and Schulenberg, whom he created Countess of Darlington and Duchess of Kendal. The Duchess was tall, and lean of stature, and hence was irreverently nicknamed the Maypole. The Countess was a large-sized noblewoman, and this elevated personage was denominated the Elephant. Both of these ladies loved Hanover and its delights; clung round the linden-trees of the great Herrenhausen avenue, and at first would not quit the place. Schulenberg, in fact, could not come on account of her debts; but finding the Maypole would not come, the Elephant packed up her

Georg. König v. England

Sophia Dorothea of Celle by
Jacques Vaillant

trunk and slipped out of Hanover unwieldy as she was. On this the Maypole straightway put herself in motion, and followed her beloved George Louis.

Take what you can get, was the old monarch's maxim. He was not a lofty monarch, certainly; he was not a patron of the fine arts; but he was not a hypocrite, he was not revengeful, he was not extravagant. Though a despot in Hanover, he was a moderate ruler in England. His aim was to leave it to itself as much as possible, and to live out of it as much as he could. His heart was in Hanover. He was more than fifty years of age when he came amongst us: we took him because we wanted him, because he served our turn; we laughed at his uncouth German ways, and sneered at him. He took our loyalty for what it was worth; laid hands on what money he could; kept us assuredly from Popery and woodenshoes. I, for one, would have been on his side in those days. Cynical, and selfish, as he was, he was better than a king out of St Germains with the French King's orders in his pocket, and a swarm of Jesuits in his train.

There are stains in the portrait for the first George, and traits in it which none of us need admire; but, among the nobler features are justice, courage, moderation – and these we may recognize ere we turn the picture to the wall.

From Thackeray *The Four Georges*.

All the Hanoverian kings had trouble with either wife or son; George I had both. His son, who became George II, set a pattern for the Hanoverian sons of detesting their fathers and becoming the focus for both political opposition and a rival social centre.

I see from your memorandum of the seventh of this month, that Your Majesty's information as to the degree to which the Prince of Wales is committed to the Tories and is against the Whigs has been grossly exaggerated, for it does not take into consideration that he has neither the liberty nor the inclination for this sort of thing.

He has not the liberty, because he has to submit to the King and tell him everything; his conduct is subject to more severe scrutiny than is that of lesser folk; he may not even employ a footman without HM's approval; how much less would he be permitted to join a party which opposed the King.

But it is true that a coldness between the prince and the King exists. They do not speak to each other; they do not visit each other's rooms; they have never eaten together; they have never been in either the same palace or private house together at the same time, nor have they been seen to walk together or attend the same hunt. It is true that they meet at the council or in chapel or at the princess's evening parties, but they do not speak. It does seem clear that this coldness originated before their arrival here since nothing has happened here to cause it.

From a letter by Bonet to the King of Prussia.

George's relationship with his father exemplifies the
Hanoverians' inability to get on with each other.

George II by Robert Pine

'I am Sir Robert Walpole,' said the messenger. The
awakened sleeper hated Sir Robert Walpole. 'I have the
honour to announce to your Majesty that your royal father,
King George I, died at Osnaburg on Saturday last, the
18th inst.'

'Dat is one big lie!' roared out his sacred Majesty King
George II; but Sir Robert Walpole stated the fact, and from
that day until three and thirty years after, George, the
second of the name, ruled over England.

How the king made away with his father's will under the
astonished nose of the Archbishop of Canterbury; how he
was a choleric little sovereign; how he shook his fist in the
face of his father's courtiers; how he kicked his coat and
wig about in his rages, and called everybody thief, liar,
rascal, with whom he differed: you will read in all the
history books; and how he speedily and shrewdly reconciled
himself with the bold minister, whom he had hated during
his father's life, and by whom he was served during
fifteen years of his own with admirable prudence, fidelity,
and success. But for Sir Robert Walpole, we should have
had the Pretender back again.

From Thackeray *The Four Georges*.

George was married to Caroline of Ansbach, a lively,
educated, intelligent woman to whom he was devoted
although he had mistresses. She dominated the King as
well as the politicians during his reign, and her death
caused him genuine grief. He directed in his will that
when he died his coffin should be placed beside hers.

I must now as well as I can connect the particulars of the
most melancholy fortnight I ever passed in my life.

On Wednesday, the 9th of November, the Queen was
taken ill and called her complaint the colic. I, imagining
her pain to proceed from a goutish humour in her stomach,
told her nothing ever gave immediate ease but strong
things. To which the Queen replied: 'Pshaw! You think
that this is the pain of an old nasty stinking gout. But I have
an ill which nobody knows of.' She then retired, going
immediately into bed, where she grew worse every
moment.

On Friday the King sent for Ranby the surgeon, and bid
him examine her. When he had done so, Ranby went and
spoke softly to the King at the chimney, upon which the
Queen started up, and said: 'I am sure now, you lying fool,
you are telling the King I have a rupture.' 'I am so,' said
Ranby, 'and Your Majesty has concealed it too long.' The
Queen made no answer, but lay down again, turning her
head to the other side, and as the King told me, he thinks it
was the only tear he saw her shed whilst she was ill.

I do firmly believe she carried her abhorrence to being
known to have a rupture so far that she would have died
without declaring it, and though people may think this
weakness little of a piece with the greatness of her character,
she knew better than anybody else that her power over the
King was not preserved independent of the charms of her
person.

On Wednesday morning she sent for Sir Robert Walpole,
who saw her alone. As soon as he came out of the room
he said: 'If ever I heard a corpse speak, it was just now
in that room. Oh! My Lord,' said he, 'If this woman should
die, who can tell into what hands the King will fall? Or who
will have the management of him?' 'For my own part'
I replied, 'I have not the least doubt how it will be. He will
cry for her for a fortnight, forget her in a month, and have
two or three women that he will pass his time with to lie
with now and then; but whilst they have most of his time,
and no power, you will have all the credit, and govern him
more absolutely than ever you did.'

About four o'clock the following morning, the Queen complained that her pain was extreme. She then took a ruby ring off her finger, and putting it upon his, said: 'This is the last thing I have to give you – naked I came to you, and naked I go from you.' She then gave it as her advice, that in case she died, the King should marry again; upon which his sobs began to rise and his tears to fall, and in the midst of this passion, with much ado he got out this answer: 'Non – j'aurai – des – maîtresses.' To which the Queen made no other reply than: 'Ah! mon Dieu! cela n'empêche pas.'

On Wednesday some wise, some pious, and a great many busy, meddling, impertinent people about the Court asking in whispers everybody they met whether the Queen had had anybody to pray by her, and wondering at the irreligion of the Queen for thinking she could pray as well for herself as anybody could pray for her, and at those about her for not putting her in mind of so essential a duty, Sir Robert Walpole desired Princess Emily to propose to the King or Queen that the Archbishop should be sent for, in order to stop people's impertinence upon this subject; and when the Princess Emily made some difficulty about taking upon her to make this proposal to the King or Queen, Sir Robert in the presence of a dozen people very prudently added, by way of stimulating the Princess Emily: 'Pray, madam, let this farce be played. The Archbiship will act it very well. You may bid him be as short as he will. It will do the Queen no hurt, no more than any good; and it will satisfy all the wise and good fools, who will call us all atheists if we don't pretend to be as great fools as they are.'

During this time the King talked perpetually to Lord Hervey, the physicians and surgeons, and his children, who were the only people he ever saw out of the Queen's room, of the Queen's good qualities, his fondness for her, his anxiety for her welfare, and the irreparable loss her death would be to him; and repeated every day, and many times in the day, all her merits in every capacity in regard to him and every other body she had to do with. He said she was the best wife, the best mother, the best companion, the best friend, and the best woman that ever was born.

These were the terms in which he was for ever now talking of the Queen, and in which he likewise talked to her; and yet so unaccountable were the sudden sallies of his temper, and so little was he able or willing to command them, that in the midst of all this flow of tenderness he hardly ever went into her room that he did not, even in

Caroline of Ansbach from the studio of C. Jervas

this moving situation, snub her for something or other she said or did. When her constant uneasiness, from the sickness in her stomach, and the soreness of her wound, made her shift her posture every minute, he would say to her: 'How the devil should you sleep, when you will never lie still a moment? You want to rest, and the doctors tell you nothing can do you so much good, and yet you are always moving about. Nobody can sleep in that manner, and that is always your way; you never take the proper method to get what you want, and then you wonder you have it not.'

And as the doctors said she might eat or drink anything she had a mind to or could swallow, the King was ever proposing something or other, which she never refused, though she knew it would only lie burning in her stomach for half an hour or an hour and then come up again. When she could get things down, notwithstanding these effects (which to other people she said she knew they would have), her complaisance to him made her always swallow them; and when he thanked her for so doing, she used to answer: 'It is the last service I can do for you.' But when her stomach recoiled so that it was impossible for her to force anything down her throat which he had given her, and that she only tasted it and gave it away, he used peevishly to say: 'How is it possible you should not know whether you like a thing or not? If you do not like it, why do you call for it; and if you do, why will you give it away?' To which she would only answer: 'I am very silly and very whimsical, for a dégoût takes me in a moment, for which I think a minute before I have a mind to.'

The two following days she grew perceptibly weaker every hour. About ten o'clock on Sunday night, the King being asleep on the floor at the feet of her bed, the Queen began to rattle in the throat. All she said before she died was 'I have now got an asthma. Open the window.'

The King kissed the face and hands of the lifeless body several times. The grief he felt for the Queen showed a tenderness of which the world thought him before utterly incapable, and made him for some time more popular and better spoken of than he had ever been before this incident, or than I believe he ever will be again.

From Lord Hervey *Memoirs of the Reign of George II.*

Do you know, I had the curiosity to go to the burying t'other night; I had never seen a royal funeral; nay, I walked as a rag of quality, which I found would be, and so it was, the easiest way of seeing it. It is absolutely a noble sight. The Prince's chamber, hung with purple, and a quantity of silver lamps, the coffin under a canopy of purple velvet, and six vast chandeliers of silver on high stands, had a very good effect. The procession, through a line of footguards, every seventh man bearing a torch, the horse-guards lining the outside, their officers with drawn sabres and crepe sashes on horseback, the drums muffled, the fifes, bells tolling, and minute guns, – all this was very solemn.

But the charm was the entrance of the Abbey, where we were received by the Dean and Chapter in rich robes, the choir and almsmen bearing torches; the whole Abbey so illuminated, that one saw it to greater advantage than by day; the tombs, long aisles, and fretted roof, all appearing distinctly, and with the happiest chiaroscuro. There wanted nothing but incense, and little chapels, here and there with priests saying mass for the repose of the defunct; yet one could not complain of its not being catholic enough. When we came to the chapel of Henry the Seventh, all solemnity and decorum ceased; no order was observed, people sat or stood where they could or would; the yeomen of the guard were crying out for help, oppressed by the immense weight of the coffin; the Bishop read sadly, and blundered in the prayers; the fine chapter, *Man that is born of a woman*, was chanted, not read; and the anthem, besides being immeasurably tedious, would have served as well for a nuptial.

The real serious part was the figure of the Duke of Cumberland, heightened by a thousand melancholy circumstances. He had a dark brown adonis, and a cloak of black cloth, with a train of five yards. Attending the funeral of a father could not be pleasant: his leg extremely bad, yet forced to stand upon it near two hours; his face bloated and distorted with his late paralytic stroke, which has affected, too, one of his eyes, and placed over the mouth of the vault, into which, in all probability, he must himself so soon descend; think how unpleasant a situation!

He bore it all with a firm and unaffected countenance. This grave scene was fully contrasted by the burlesque Duke of Newcastle. He fell into a fit of crying the moment he came into the chapel, and flung himself back in a stall, the Archbishop hovering over him with a smelling-bottle; but in two minutes his curiosity got the better of his hypocrisy,

and he ran about the chapel with his glass to spy who was
or was not there, spying with one hand, and mopping his
eyes with the other. Then returned the fear of catching
cold; and the Duke of Cumberland, who was sinking with
heat, felt himself weighed down, and turning round, found
it was the Duke of Newcastle standing upon his train, to
avoid the chill of the marble. It was very theatric to look
down into the vault, where the coffin lay, attended by
mourners with lights. Clavering, the groom of the
bedchamber, refused to sit up with the body, and was
dismissed by the King's order.

The new reign dates with great propriety and decency.
Holinshed or Baker would think it begins well. The young
King has all the appearance of being amiable. There is
extreme good nature, which breaks out on all occasions. He
doesn't stand in one spot, with his eyes fixed royally on the
ground, and dropping bits of German news: he walks
about and speaks to everybody. All his speeches are obliging.
If they do as well behind the scenes, as upon the stage, it
will be a very complete reign.

From a letter by Horace Walpole.

**Poor George III was ill and mad though he had
intermittent periods of sanity. The novelist and diarist,
Fanny Burney, had two brushes with him:**

Well, dear Mrs Delany beseeched me: 'I do beg of you,'
she said 'when the Queen or the King speaks to you, not to
answer with mere monosyllables. The Queen often
complains to me of the difficulty with which she can get
any conversation, as she not only always has to start the
subjects, but commonly entirely to support them: and she
says there is nothing she so much loves as conversation, and
nothing she finds so hard to get.' This was a most tremendous
injunction; however, I could not but promise her I would
do the best I could.

The door of the drawing-room was again opened, and a
large man, in deep mourning, appeared at it, entering and
shutting it himself without speaking.

   A ghost could not more have scared me, when I discovered
by the glitter on the black, a star! The general disorder had
prevented his being seen, except by myself, who was
always on the watch, till Miss P——, turning round,
exclaimed: 'The King! – Aunt, the King!'

   O mercy! thought I, that I were but out of the room!
Which way shall I escape? And how to pass him unnoticed?
There is but the single door at which he entered, in the
room! Every one scampered out of the way: Miss P——, to
stand next the door; Mr Bernard Dewes to a corner
opposite it; his little girl clung to me; and Mrs Delany
advanced to meet his Majesty, who, after quietly looking
on till she saw him, approached, and inquired how she did.

   He then spoke to Mr Bernard, whom he had already met
two or three times here.

   I had now retreated to the wall, and purposed gliding
softly, though speedily, out of the room; but before I had
taken a single step, the King, in a loud whisper to Mrs
Delany, said: 'Is that Miss Burney?' and on her answering:
'Yes, sir,' he bowed, and with a countenance of the most
perfect good humour, came close up to me.

   A most profound reverence on my part arrested the
progress of my intended retreat.

   'How long have you been come back, Miss Burney?'

   'Two days, sir.'

   Unluckily he did not hear me, and repeated his question;
and whether the second time he heard me or not, I don't

know, but he made a little civil inclination of his head, and
went back to Mrs Delany.

He insisted she should sit down, though he stood himself,
and began to give her an account of the Princess Elizabeth,
who once again was recovering, and trying, at present,
James's Powders. She had been blooded, he said, twelve
times in this last fortnight, and had lost seventy-five ounces
of blood, besides undergoing blistering and other discipline.
He spoke of her illness with the strongest emotion, and
seemed quite filled with concern for her danger and
sufferings.

Mrs Delany next inquired for the younger children. They
had all, he said, the whooping-cough, and were soon to be
removed to Kew.

A good deal of talk then followed about his own health,
and the extreme temperance by which he preserved it. The
fault of his constitution, he said, was a tendency to excessive
fat, which he kept, however, in order by the most vigorous
exercise, and the strictest attention to a simple diet.

When Mrs Delany was beginning to praise his forbear-
ance, he stopped her.

'No, no,' he cried, ''tis no virtue; I only prefer eating plain
and little, to growing diseased and infirm.'

When the discourse upon health and strength was over,
the King went up to the table, and looked at a book of
prints, from Claude Lorraine. He turned over a leaf or
two, and then said: 'Pray, does Miss Burney draw, too?'

The too was pronounced very civilly.

'I believe not, sir,' answered Mrs Delany; 'at least, she
does not tell.'

'Oh!' cried he, laughing, 'that's nothing! She is not apt to
tell; she never does tell, you know! Her father told me that
himself. He told me the whole history of her *Evelina*. And I
shall never forget his face when he spoke of his feelings at
first taking up the book! – he looked quite frightened, just
as if he was doing it that moment! I never can forget his
face while I live!'

Then coming up close to me, he said:

'But what? – what? – how was it?'

'Sir,' cried I, not well understanding him.

'How came you – how happened it? – what? – what?'

'I – I only wrote, sir, for my own amusement – only in
some odd, idle hours.'

'But your publishing – your printing – how was that?'

'That was only, sir – only because ——.' I hesitated most
abominably, not knowing how to tell him a long story, and
growing terribly confused at these questions.

The What? was then repeated with so earnest a look, that, forced to say something, I stammeringly answered. 'I thought – sir – it would look very well in print!'

I do really flatter myself this is the silliest speech I ever made! I am quite provoked with myself for it; but a fear of laughing made me eager to utter anything, and by no means conscious, till I had spoken, of what I was saying.

He laughed very heartily himself – well he might – and walked away to enjoy it, crying out: 'Very fair indeed! That's being very fair and honest!'

Then, returning to me again, he said: 'But your father – how came you not to show him what you wrote?'

'I was too much ashamed of it, sir, seriously.' Literal truth that, I am sure.

While this was talking over, a violent thunder was made at the door. I was almost certain it was the Queen. Once more I would have given anything to escape; but in vain. I had been informed that nobody ever quitted the royal presence, after having been conversed with, till motioned to withdraw.

Miss P——, according to established etiquette on these occasions, opened the door which she stood next, by putting her hand behind her, and slid out backwards into the hall, to light the Queen in. The door soon opened again, and her Majesty entered.

Immediately seeing the King, she made him a low curtsy, and cried: 'Oh, your Majesty is here!'

'Yes,' he cried, 'I ran here without speaking to anybody.'

The Queen then hastened up to Mrs Delany, with both her hands held out, saying: 'My dear Mrs Delany, how are you?'

She made Mrs Delany sit next her, and Miss P—— brought her some tea.

The King, meanwhile, came to me again, and said: 'Are you musical?'

'Not a performer, sir.'

Then, going from me to the Queen, he cried: 'She does not play.'

I did not hear what the Queen answered; she spoke in a low voice, and seemed much out of spirits.

The King then returned to me, and said: 'Are you sure you never play? Never touch the keys at all?'

'Never to acknowledge it, sir.'

'Oh! that's it!' cried he; and flying to the Queen, cried: 'She does play – but not to acknowledge it!'

I was now in a most horrible panic once more; pushed so very home, I could answer no other than I did, for these categorical questions almost constrain categorical answers; and here, at Windsor, it seems an absolute point that whatever they ask must be told, and whatever they desire must be done. Think but, then, of my consternation, in expecting their commands to perform!

The eager air with which he returned to me fully explained what was to follow. I hastily, therefore, spoke first, in order to stop him, crying: 'I never sir, played to anybody but myself! Never!'

'No? Are you sure?' cried he, disappointed; 'but – but you'll ——.'

'I have never, sir,' cried I, very earnestly, 'played in my life, but when I could hear nobody else – quite alone, and from a mere love of any musical sounds.'

He still, however, kept me in talk, and still upon music.

'To me,' said he, 'it appears quite as strange to meet with people who have no ear for music, and cannot distinguish one air from another, as to meet with people who are dumb. Lady Bell Finch once told me that she had heard there was some difference between a psalm, a minuet, and a country dance, but she declared they all sounded alike to her! There are people who have no eye for difference of colour. The Duke of Marlborough actually cannot tell scarlet from green!'

The sermon of the day before was then talked over. Some time afterwards the King said he found by the newspapers that Mrs Clive was dead. Do you read the newspapers, thought I? Oh, King, you must then have the most unvexing temper in the world not to run wild.

This led on to more players. He was sorry, he said, for the Hendersons, and the more as Mrs Siddons had wished to have him play at the same house with herself.

Then Mrs Siddons took her turn, and with the warmest praise.

'I am an enthusiast for her', cried the King, 'quite an enthusiast. I think there was never any player in my time so excellent – not Garrick himself; I own it!'

Then coming close to me, who was silent he said: 'What? what?' – meaning 'What say you?' But I still said nothing. I could not concur where I thought so differently, and to enter into an argument was quite impossible; for every little thing the King listened to with an eagerness that made me always ashamed of its insignificancy. And, indeed, but for that I should have talked to him with much greater fluency, as well as ease.

From players he went to plays, and complained of the
great want of good modern comedies, and of the extreme
immorality of most of the old ones. Then he specified
several; but I had read none of them and could say nothing
about the matter – till, at last he came to Shakespeare.

'Was there ever,' cried he, 'such stuff as great part of
Shakespeare? only one must not say so! But what think
you? – what? – Is there not sad stuff? – what? – what?'

'Yes, indeed, I think so, sir, though mixed with such
excellences, that –'. 'Oh,' cried he, laughing good
humouredly, 'I know it is not to be said! but it's true. Only
it's Shakespeare, and nobody dare abuse him.'

What an adventure had I this morning! one that has
occasioned me the severest personal terror I ever experienced in my life.

Sir Lucas Pepys persisting that exercise and air were
absolutely necessary to save me from illness, I have
continued my walks, varying my gardens from Richmond
to Kew, according to the accounts I received of the move-
ments of the King.

This morning, when I received my intelligence of the
King from Dr John Willis, I begged to know where I might
walk in safety? 'In Kew Gardens,' he said, 'as the King
would be in Richmond.'

'Should any unfortunate circumstance,' I cried, 'at any
time, occasion my being seen by his Majesty, do not
mention my name, but let me run off without call or
notice.'

This he promised. Everybody, indeed, is ordered to keep
out of sight.

Taking, therefore, the time I had most at command,
I strolled into the gardens. I had proceeded, in my quick
way, nearly half the round, when I suddenly perceived,
through some trees, two or three figures. Relying on the
instructions of Dr John, I concluded them to be workmen
and gardeners; yet tried to look sharp, and in so doing, as
they were less shaded, I thought I saw the person of his
Majesty!

Alarmed past all possible expression, I waited not to
know more, but turning back, ran off with all my might.
But what was my terror to hear myself pursued – to hear
the voice of the King himself loudly and hoarsely calling
after me: 'Miss Burney! Miss Burney!'

I protest I was ready to die. I knew not in what state he
might be at the time; I only knew the orders to keep out of

his way were universal; on I ran, too terrified to stop, and in search of some short passage, for the garden is full of little labyrinths, by which I might escape.

The steps still pursued me, and still the poor hoarse and altered voice rang in my ears – more and more footsteps resounded frightfully behind me – the attendants all running, to catch their eager master.

Heavens, how I ran! I do not think I should have felt the hot lava from Vesuvius – at least not the hot cinders – had I so run during its eruption. My feet were not sensible that they even touched the ground.

Soon after, I heard other voices, shriller, though less nervous, call out: 'Stop! Stop! Stop!'

I could by no means consent; I knew not what was purposed, but I recollected fully my agreement with Dr John that very morning, that I should decamp if surprised, and not be named.

My own fears and repugnance, also, after a flight and disobedience like this, were doubled in the thought of not escaping: I knew not to what I might be exposed, should the malady be then high, and take the turn of resentment. Still, therefore, on I flew; and such was my speed, so almost incredible to relate or recollect, that I fairly believe no one of the whole party could have overtaken me, if these words, from one of the attendants, had not reached me: 'Doctor Willis begs you to stop!'

'I cannot! I cannot!' I answered, still flying on, when he called out: 'You must, ma'am; it hurts the King to run.'

Then, indeed, I stopped – in a state of fear really amounting to agony. I turned round, I saw the two Doctors had got the King between them, and three attendants of Dr Willis's were hovering about.

As they approached, some little presence of mind happily came to my command: it occurred to me that, to appease the wrath of my flight, I must now show some confidence: I therefore faced them as undauntedly as I was able.

When they were within a few yards of me, the King called out: 'Why did you run away?'

Shocked at a question impossible to answer, yet a little assured by the mild tone of his voice, I instantly forced myself forward, to meet him, though the internal sensation, which satisfied me this was a step the most proper to appease his suspicions and displeasure, was so violently combated by the tremor of my nerves, that I fairly think I may reckon it the greatest effort of personal courage I have ever made.

Charlotte of Mecklenburg-Strelitz by Peter Edward Stroehling

*George IV as Prince Regent
by Sir Thomas Lawrence*

The effort answered: I looked up, and met all his unwonted benignity of countenance, though something still of wildness in his eyes. Think, however, of my surprise, to feel him put both his hands round my two shoulders, and then kiss my cheek!

He now spoke in such terms of his pleasure in seeing me, that I soon lost the whole of my terror; astonishment to find him so nearly well, and gratification to see him so pleased, removed every uneasy feeling, and the joy that succeeded, in my conviction of his recovery, made me ready to throw myself at his feet to express it.

What a conversation followed!

A link with George and his madness is provided by a letter the novelist E. M. Forster, who only died in 1970, received when a small boy from his aunt Marianne Thornton.

Dear Master Morgan,

I think it's time now for you to write me another letter. Do you write every day? I can show you a big thick copy-book that when I was just your age I wrote for my father. And what do you think he did to reward me? Why, poor old George the Third was coming to summon Parliament. He was a good man and wanted to do right, but he was very obstinate and used to get very angry and at last very ill, and he quite lost his senses and kept calling the people about him peacocks.

When the day came for him to meet his faithful commons, though very ill, he insisted on having his own way, so they gave it him, and he went, and I could see his carriage – all gold and glass, and I did so beg of papa to let me go across Palace Yard, and he carried me across and took me into the House of Commons. And there he was sitting on the Throne with his King's Crown on, his robes scarlet and ermine, and held his speech written out for him, just what he had to say. But, oh dear, he strode up and made a bow and began 'My Lords and Peacocks'.

The people who were not fond of him laughed, the people who did love him cried, and he went back to be no longer a King, and his eldest son reigned in his stead, and Regent Street was named after him.

George was made Regent in 1811 and ruled for nine
years until his father died. His grossness and extravagance
provoked much hatred and satire in an age when the
gathering momentum of the industrial revolution brought
many social discontents in its train.

The King's indolence is so great that it is next to impossible
to get him to do even the most ordinary business and
Knighton is still the only man who can prevail on him to
sign papers, etc. His greatest delight is to make those who
have business to transact with him, or to lay papers before
him, wait in his anteroom while he is lounging with Mount
Charles or anybody, talking of horses or any trivial matter;
and when he is told, 'Sir, there is Watson waiting etc,' he
replies, 'Damn Watson; let him wait.' He does it on purpose
and likes it.

This account corresponds with all I have before heard,
and confirms the opinion I have long had that a more
contemptible, cowardly, selfish, unfeeling dog, does not
exist than this king, on whom such flattery is constantly
lavished. He has a sort of capricious good-nature, arising
however out of no good principle or good feeling, but
which is of use to him, as it cancels in a moment and at
small cost a long score of misconduct. Princes have only to
behave with common decency and prudence, and they are
sure to be popular, for there is a great and general
disposition to pay court to them. I do not know anybody
who is proof against their seductions when they think fit to
use them in the shape of civility and condescension. The
great consolation in all this is the proof that, so far from
deriving happiness from their grandeur, they are the most
miserable of all mankind. The contrast between their
apparent authority and the contradictions which they
practically meet with must be peculiarly galling, more
especially to men whose minds are seldom regulated, as
other men's are, by the beneficial discipline of education
and early collision with their equals. There have been good
and wise kings, but not many of them. The littleness of his
character prevents his displaying the dangerous faults that
belong to great minds, but with vices and weaknesses of the
lowest and most contemptible order it would be difficult to
find a disposition more abundantly furnished.

He leads a most extraordinary life – never gets up till
six in the afternoon. They come to him and open the
window curtains at six or seven o'clock in the morning; he
breakfasts in bed, does whatever business he can be brought

George IV from the studio of Sir Thomas Lawrence

to transact in bed too, he reads every newspaper quite through, dozes three or four hours, gets up in time for dinner, and goes to bed between ten and eleven. He sleeps very ill, and rings his bell forty times in the night; if he wants to know the hour, though a watch hangs close to him, he will have his valet de chambre down rather than turn his head to look at it. The same thing if he wants a glass of water; he won't stretch out his hand to get it. His valets are nearly destroyed.

From Charles Greville *Memoirs.*

George in his youth had married Maria Fitzherbert but it suited him ten years later to deny it, particularly when Parliament offered to pay his debts on his marriage to Caroline of Brunswick. When he saw her he said 'I am not well, get me a glass of brandy'. The marriage was a disaster and they parted a few months later, after George had written letters in this vein.

Madam,

As Lord Cholmondeley informs me that you wish I would define, in writing, the terms upon which we are to live, I shall endeavour to explain myself with as much clearness, and with as much propriety as the nature of the subject will admit. Our inclinations are not in our power, nor should either of us be held answerable to the other, because nature has not made us suitable to each other. Tranquil and comfortable society is, however, in our power; let our intercourse, therefore, be restricted to that, and I will distinctly subscribe to the condition which you required, through Lady Cholmondeley, that even in the event of any accident happening to my daughter, which I trust Providence in his mercy will avert, I shall not infringe the terms of the restriction by proposing at any period, a connexion of a more particular nature. I shall now finally close this disagreeable correspondence trusting that as we have completely explained ourselves to each other, the rest of our lives will be passed in uninterrupted tranquility.

But more was to come; Caroline was vulgar, coarse and profligate. She lived abroad for a time causing great

scandal in Italy, and on her return to England at
George III's death, George IV sued for a divorce, the trial
for which took place in the House of Lords. The bill was
eventually withdrawn, but Caroline's final humiliation was
being turned away from the doors of Westminster
Abbey where she presented herself expecting to be
crowned queen at George's coronation.
George himself did not escape criticism.

To make a portrait of him at first seemed a matter of small
difficulty. There is his coat, his star, his wig, his countenance
simpering under it: with a slate and a piece of chalk, I could
at this very desk perform a recognizable likeness of him.
And yet after reading of him in scores of volumes, hunting
him through old magazines and newspapers, having him
here at a ball, there at a public dinner, there at races and so
forth, you find you have nothing – nothing but a coat and
a wig and a mask smiling below it – nothing but a great
simulacrum. His sires and grandsires were men. One knows
what they were like: what they would do in given
circumstances: that on occasion they fought and demeaned
themselves like tough good soldiers. The sailor King who
came after George was a man: the Duke of York was a
man, big, burly, loud, jolly, cursing, courageous. But this
George, what was he? I look through all his life, and
recognise but a bow and a grin. I try to take him to pieces,
and find silk stockings, padding, stays, a coat with frogs and
a fur collar, a star and blue ribbon, a pocket-handkerchief
prodigiously scented, one of Truefitt's best nutty-brown
wigs reeking with oil, a set of teeth and a huge black stock,
underwaistcoats, more underwaistcoats, and then nothing.
I know of no sentiment that he ever distinctly uttered.
Documents are published under his name, but people
wrote them – private letters, but people spelt them. He put
a great George P. or George R. at the bottom of the page
and fancied he had written the paper; some bookseller's
clerk, some poor author, some man did the work; saw to
the spelling, cleaned up the slovenly sentences, and gave
the lax maudlin slipslop a sort of consistency. About
George, one can get at nothing actual. That outside, I am
certain, is pad and tailor's work; there may be something
behind, but what? We cannot get at the character; no doubt
never shall. Will men of the future have nothing better to
do than to unswathe and interpret that Royal old mummy?

   His biographers say that when he commenced house-
keeping in that splendid new palace of his, the Prince of

Wales had some windy projects of encouraging literature, science, and the arts; of having assemblies of literary characters; and societies for the encouragement of geography, astronomy, and botany. Astronomy, geography, and botany! Fiddlesticks! French ballet-dancers, French cooks, horse-jockeys, buffoons, procurers, tailors, boxers, fencing-masters, china, jewel, and gimcrack merchants – these were his real companions.

His natural companions were dandies and parasites. He could talk to a tailor or a cook; but, as the equal of great statesmen, to set up a creature, lazy, weak, indolent, besotted, of monstrous vanity, and levity incurable – it is absurd. They thought to use him, and did for a while; but they must have known how timid he was; how entirely heartless and treacherous, and have expected his desertion. His next set of friends were mere table companions, of whom he grew tired too; then we hear of him with a very few select toadies, mere boys from school or the Guards, whose sprightliness tickled the fancy of the worn-out voluptuary. What matters what friends he had? He dropped all his friends, he never could have real friends. An heir to the throne has flatterers, adventurers who hang about him, ambitious men who use him; but friendship is denied him.

The great war of empires and giants goes on. Day by day victories are won and lost by the brave. Torn smoky flags and battered eagles are wrenched from the heroic enemy and laid at his feet; and he sits there on his throne and smiles, and gives the guerdon of valour to the conqueror. I believe it is certain about George IV, that he had heard so much of the war, knighted so many people, and worn such a prodigious quantity of marshal's uniforms, cocked-hats, cock's feathers, scarlet and bullion in general, that he actually fancied he had been present in some campaigns, and, under the name of General Brock, led a tremendous charge of the German legion at Waterloo.

He is dead but thirty years, and one asks how a great society could have tolerated him? Would we bear him now? In this quarter of a century, what a silent revolution has been working! how it has separated us from old times and manners! How it has changed men themselves! I can see old gentlemen now among us, of perfect good breeding, of quiet lives, with venerable grey heads, fondling their grandchildren; and look at them, and wonder what they were once.

What a strange Court! What a queer privacy of morals and manners do we look into! Shall we regard it as preachers and moralists, and cry Woe, against the open

Overleaf
The trial of Caroline of Brunswick-Wolfenbuttel in the House of Lords by Sir George Hayter

vice and selfishness and corruption; or look at it as we do at the king in the pantomine, with his pantomime wife and pantomime courtiers, whose big heads he knocks together, whom he pokes with his pantomime sceptre, whom he orders to prison under the guard of his pantomime beefeaters, as he sits down to dine on his pantomime pudding? It is grave, it is sad: it is a theme most curious for moral and political speculation; it is monstrous, grotesque, laughable, with its prodigious littlenesses, etiquettes, ceremonials, sham moralities; it is as serious as a sermon; and as absurd and outrageous as Punch's puppet show.

He the first gentleman of Europe! There is no stronger satire on the proud English society of that day, than that they admired George.

From Thackeray *The Four Georges*.

William IV was George IV's brother. He was nearly sixty-nine when he succeeded, a bluff, genial man known as 'Sailor Bill' since he had served for a time in the navy and acquired a taste for naval language.

The middle-class tendencies of the monarchy became very pronounced during his reign and he did much to rescue the crown from the obloquy it had earned under his brother.

The present King and his proceedings occupy all attention, and nobody thinks any more of the late King than if he had been dead fifty years, unless it be to abuse him and to rake up all his vices and misdeeds. Never was elevation like that of King William IV. His life has been hitherto passed in obscurity and neglect, in miserable poverty, surrounded by a numerous progeny of bastards.

King George had not been dead three days before everybody discovered that he was no loss, and King William a great gain. Certainly nobody ever was less regretted than the late King, and the breath was hardly out of his body before the press burst forth in full cry against him, and raked up all his vices, follies, and misdeeds, which were numerous and glaring enough.

The new King began very well. His first speech to the Council was well enough given, but his burlesque character began even then to show itself. Nobody expected from him much real grief, and he does not seem to know how to act it consistently; he spoke of his brother with all the semblance of feeling, and in a tone of voice properly softened and subdued, but just afterwards, when they gave him the pen to sign the declaration, he said, in his usual tone, 'This is a damned bad pen you have given me.'

A few days after my return I was sworn in, all the Ministers and some others being present. His Majesty presided very decently, and looked like a respectable old admiral. The Duke of Wellington told me he was delighted with him – 'If I had been able to deal with my late master as I do with my present, I should have got on much better' – that he was so reasonable and tractable, and that he had done more business with him in ten minutes than with the other in as many days.

He began immediately to do good-natured things; the great offices of Chamberlain and Steward he abandoned to the Duke of Wellington. There never was anything like the

enthusiasm with which he was greeted by all ranks;
though he has trotted about both town and country for
sixty-four years, and nobody ever turned round to look at
him, he cannot stir now without a mob, patrician as well as
plebeian, at his heels. All the Park congregated round the
gate to see him drive into town the day before yesterday.
But in the midst of all this success and good conduct certain
indications of strangeness and oddness peep out which are
not a little alarming, and he promises to realise the fears of
his Ministers that he will do and say too much, though they
flatter themselves that they have muzzled him in his
approaching progress by reminding him that his words
will be taken as his Ministers', and he must, therefore, be
chary of them.

At the late King's funeral, he behaved with great
indecency. That ceremony was very well managed, and a
fine sight, the military part particularly, and the Guards
were magnificent. The attendance was not very numerous,
and when they had all got together in St George's Hall a
gayer company I never beheld; with the exception of
Mount Charles, who was deeply affected, they were all as
merry as grigs. The King was chief mourner, and, to my
astonishment, as he entered the chapel directly behind the
body, in a situation in which he should have been apparently,
if not really, absorbed in the melancholy duty he was
performing, he darted up to Strathaven, who was ranged
on one side below the Dean's stall, shook him heartily by
the hand, and then went on nodding to the right and left.

The King's good-nature, simplicity, and affability to all
about him are very striking, and in his elevation he does not
forget any of his old friends and companions. He was in no
hurry to take upon himself the dignity of King nor to throw
off the habits and manners of a country gentleman.
Altogether he seems a kind-hearted, well-meaning, not
stupid, burlesque, bustling old fellow, and if he doesn't go
mad may make a very decent King, but he exhibits oddities.
All odd, and people are frightened, but his wits will at
least last till the new Parliament meets.

All this was very well; no great harm in it; more affable,
less dignified than the late King; but when this was over,
and he might very well have sat down and rested, he must
needs put on his plainer clothes and start on a ramble about
the streets, alone too. In Pall Mall he met Watson Taylor,
and took his arm and went up St James's Street. There he
was soon followed by a mob making an uproar, and when
he got near White's a woman came up and kissed him.
When he got home he asked them to go in and take a quiet

William IV by M. A. Shee

walk in the garden, and said, 'Oh, never mind all this; when
I have walked about a few times they will get used to it,
and will take no notice.'

The other night the King had a party, and at eleven
o'clock he dismissed them thus: 'Now, ladies and
gentlemen, I wish you a good night. I will not detain you
any longer from your amusements, and shall go to my own,
which is to go to bed; so come along, my Queen.' The other
day he was very angry because the guard did not know him
in his plain clothes and turn out for him – the first
appearance of jealousy of his greatness he has shown – and
he ordered them to be more on the alert for the future.

The King has been to Woolwich, inspecting the artillery,
to whom he gave a dinner, with toasts and hip, hip,
hurrahing and three times three, himself giving the time.
I tremble for him; he is only a mountebank, but he bids
fair to be a maniac.

When he arrived at Windsor and went into the drawing
room where the whole party was assembled, he went up
to the Princess Victoria, took hold of both her hands, and
expressed his pleasure at seeing her there and his regret at
not seeing her oftener. After dinner he made a very long
speech, in the course of which he poured forth the following
extraordinary and foudroyante tirade: I trust in God that
my life may be spared for nine months longer, after which
period, in the event of my death, no regency would take
place. I should then have the satisfaction of leaving the royal
authority to the personal exercise of that young lady
(pointing to the Princess), the heiress presumptive of the
Crown, and not in the hands of a person now near me, who
is surrounded by evil advisers and who is herself incom-
petent to act with propriety in the station in which she
would be placed.

No contrast can be greater than that between the
personal demeanour of the present and the late sovereigns
at their respective accessions.

The young Queen, who might well be either dazzled or
confounded with the grandeur and novelty of her
situation, seems neither the one nor the other, and behaves
with a decorum and propriety beyond her years, and with
all the sedateness and dignity the want of which was so
conspicuous in her uncle.

From Charles Greville *Memoirs*.

Adelaide of Saxe-Meiningen
by Francis Xavier Winterhalter

VICTORIA

*Victoria, aged 16 with her
spaniel Dash by Sir George
Hayter*

The young princess, granddaughter of George III,
ascended the throne at a time when the Crown had been
brought into much disrepute. Her girlish enthusiasm was
a great help in restoring its reputation.

Thursday, 28th June!

I was awoke at four o'clock by the guns in the Park, and
could not get much sleep afterwards on account of the
noise of the people, bands, etc. etc. Got up at 7 feeling
strong and well. The Park presented a curious spectacle;
crowds of people up to Constitution Hill, soldiers, bands,
etc. I dressed, having taken a little breakfast before I
dressed, and a little after. At 10 I got into the State coach
with the Duchess of Sutherland and Lord Albemarle, and
we began our Progress. It was a fine day and the crowds of
people exceeded what I have ever seen; many as there were
the day I went to the City, it was nothing – nothing to the
multitudes, the millions of my loyal subjects who were
assembled in every spot to witness the Procession. Their
good-humour and excessive loyalty was beyond everything,
and I really cannot say how proud I feel to be the Queen of
such a Nation.

   I reached the Abbey amid deafening cheers at a little
past ½ p. 11; I first went into a robing-room quite close to
the entrance, where I found my eight Train-bearers, all
dressed exactly alike and beautifully, in white satin and
silver tissue, with wreaths of silver corn-ears in front, and a
small one of pink roses round the plait behind, and pink
roses in the trimming of the dresses.

   After putting on my Mantle, and the young ladies having
properly got hold of it and Lord Conyngham holding the
end of it, I left the robing-room and the Procession began.
The sight was splendid, the bank of Peeresses quite
beautiful, all in their robes, and the Peers on the other side.
The Bishop of Durham stood on one side near me, but he
was, as Lord Melbourne told me, remarkably maladroit
and could never tell me what was to take place. At the
beginning of the Anthem where he made a mark, I retired
to St Edward's Chapel, a small dark place immediately
behind the altar with my Ladies and Train-bearers; took
off my crimson robe and kirtle and put on the supertunics
of Cloth of Gold, then proceeded bare-headed into the
Abbey; I was then seated upon St Edward's chair where the
Dalmatic robe was clasped round me by the Lord Great
Chamberlain. Then followed all the various things; and

last (of those things) the Crown being placed on my head; – which was, I must own, a most beautiful impressive moment; all the Peers and Peeresses put on their Coronets at the same instant.

My excellent Lord Melbourne, who stood very close to me throughout the whole ceremony, was completely overcome at this moment, and very much affected; he gave me such a kind, and I may say fatherly look.

The Enthronization and the Homage of, 1st, all the Bishops, then my Uncles, and lastly of all the Peers, in their respective order, was very fine. Poor old Lord Rolle, who is 82 and dreadfully infirm, in attempting to ascend the steps, fell and rolled quite down, but was not the least hurt. When Lord Melbourne's turn to do Homage came, there was loud cheering; they also cheered Lord Grey and the Duke of Wellington. It's a pretty ceremony: they first all touch the Crown, and then kiss my hand. When my good Lord Melbourne knelt down and kissed my hand, he pressed my hand and I grasped his with all my heart, at which he looked up with his eyes filled with tears and seemed very much touched, as he was, I observed, throughout the whole ceremony. After the Homage was concluded I left the throne, took off my Crown and received the sacrament; I then put on my Crown again, and re-ascended the Throne, leaning on Lord Melbourne's arm; at the commencement of the Anthem I descended from the Throne and went into St Edward's Chapel with my ladies, Train-bearers, and Lord Willoughby, where I took off the Dalmatic robe, supertunics, and put on the Purple Velvet Kirtle and Mantle, and proceeded again to the Throne, which I ascended leaning on Lord Melbourne's hand. I then again descended from the Throne, and repaired with all the Peers bearing the Regalia, my Ladies and Train-bearers, to St Edward's Chapel, as it is called; but which, as Lord Melbourne said, was more unlike a Chapel than anything he had ever seen; for, what was called an Altar was covered with sandwiches, bottles of wine, etc.

The Archbishop came and ought to have delivered the Orb to me, but I had already got it and he (as usual) was so confused and puzzled and knew nothing, and – went away. There we waited for some minutes. Lord Melbourne took a glass of wine, for he seemed completely tired; the Procession being formed, I replaced my Crown (which I had taken off for a few minutes), took the Orb in my left hand and the Sceptre in my right, and thus loaded, proceeded through the Abbey, which resounded with cheers to the first Robing-room, where I found the Duchess of Gloucester,

Mamma, and the Duchess of Cambridge, with their ladies. And here we waited for at least an hour with all my ladies and Train-Bearers. The Archbishop had (most awkwardly) put the ring on the wrong finger, and the consequence was that I had the greatest difficulty to take it off again, – which I at last did with great pain. At about $\frac{1}{2}$ p. 4 I re-entered my carriage, the Crown on my head and Sceptre and Orb in my hand and we proceeded the same way as we came – the crowds if possible having increased, the enthusiasm, affection and loyalty was really touching. I came home at a little after 6, really not feeling tired.

At 8 we dined. Lord Melbourne came up to me and said, 'I must congratulate you on this brilliant day', and that all had gone off so well. He said he was not tired and was in high spirits. I sat between uncle Ernest and Lord Melbourne. My kind Lord Melbourne was much affected in speaking of the whole ceremony. He asked kindly if I was tired, said the sword he carried (the 1st, the Sword of State) was exceedingly heavy. I said that the Crown hurt me a good deal. We agreed that the whole thing was a very fine sight. He thought the robes, and particularly the Dalmatic, 'looked remarkably well'. 'And you did it all so well; excellent!' said he, with the tears in his eyes.

After dinner, we spoke of the numbers of Peers at the Coronation, which Lord Melbourne said, with the tears in his eyes, was unprecedented. I observed that there were very few Viscounts; he said 'There are very few Viscounts', that they were an odd sort of title and not really English; that Dukes and Barons were the only real English titles; that Marquises were likewise not English; and that they made people Marquises when they did not wish to make them Dukes. I then sat on the sofa for a little while. I said to Lord Melbourne, that I felt a little tired on my feet; 'You must be very tired' he said, spoke of the weight of the robes, etc; the Coronets; and he turned round and said to me so kindly, 'And you did it beautifully, every part of it, with so much taste; it's a thing you can't give persons advice upon; it must be left to a person.' To hear this from this kind impartial friend, gave me great and real pleasure. Mamma and Feodore came back just after he said this. Spoke of these Bishops' Copes, about which he was very funny; of the Pages, who were such a nice set of boys and who were so handy, Lord Melbourne said, that they kept them near them the whole time. Little Lord Stafford and Slane (Lord Mountcharles) were pages to their fathers and looked lovely; Lord Paget (not a fine boy) was Lord Melbourne's Page and remarkably handy, he said. Spoke again of the

*Albert by Francis Xavier
Winterhalter*

young ladies' dress about which he was very amusing. He
said there was a large breakfast in the Jerusalem Chamber,
where they met before all began: he said, laughing that
whenever the Clergy or a Dean and Chapter had anything
to do with anything, there's sure to be plenty to eat. Spoke
of my intending to go to bed; he said 'You may depend
upon it, you are more tired than you think you are.'

From Victoria *Journals.*

**Victoria married Albert of Saxe-Coburg on 10 February
1840 when she was twenty-one and wrote to him on
that day:**

Dearest

How are you today, and have you slept well? I have rested
very well, and feel very comfortable today. What weather!
I believe, however, the rain will cease. Send one word when
you, my most dearly loved bridegroom will be ready.
Thy everfaithful

Victoria R

**She made him Prince Consort in 1857 and they lived
together in domesticity until his tragic death from typhoid
in 1861. Victoria was heartbroken, and wrote to her uncle,
Leopold, King of the Belgians:**

My Own, Dearest, Kindest Father:

She whom you knew as a poor fatherless baby of eight
months is now the utterly brokenhearted and crushed
widow of forty-two! Oh, to be cut off – to see our happy
life cut off so young – is too awful, too cruel. It is like losing
half of one's body and soul, torn forcibly away. His purity
was too great, his aspiration too high for this poor, miserable
world! My hero, my glorious and exceptionally great
husband! The world is gone for me, my life as a happy one
is ended. I only lived through him. My thoughts were his,
he guided and protected me, he comforted me. I can truly
say that he was my entire self, my very life and soul, even

Caricature of Victoria with
the Prince of Wales by
Max Beerbohm

my conscience. For him I would have given my life a
hundred times over, would have followed bare-foot over
the world! I live on with him, for him; in fact, I am only
outwardly separated from him, and only for a time.

Dearest, dearest Uncle, would it be possible for you to
come here for a few days, if I am still alive? I know you will
help me in this staggering darkness. It is but for a short
time, and then I go – never to part! Oh! that blessed,
blessed thought! To think of him so near to me, so quite my
own again! The longing for him, the desire to see and hear
him, to throw myself into his arms and find peace there.
Oh, God, why must it be so? This yearning is such torture!

**The Queen led an increasingly secluded life after the death
of the Prince Consort, and was taken to task for doing so
by the Editor of *The Times* in 1863. She replied to the
attack in a letter:**

An erroneous idea seems generally to prevail, and has
latterly found frequent expression in the newspapers, that
the Queen is about to resume the place in society which she
occupied before her great affliction; that is, that she is about
again to hold Levées and Drawing-Rooms in person, and to
appear as before at Court Balls, concerts, etc. This idea
cannot be too explicity contradicted.

The Queen heartily appreciates the desire of her subjects
to see her, and whatever she can do to gratify them in this
loyal and affectionate wish she will do. Whenever any
real object is to be attained by her appearing on public
occasions, any national interest to be promoted, or
anything to be encouraged which is for the good of her
people, her Majesty will not shrink, as she has not shrunk,
from any personal sacrifice or exertion, however painful.

But there are other and higher duties than those of mere
representation which are now thrown upon the Queen,
alone and unassisted – duties which she cannot neglect
without injury to the public service, which weigh
unceasingly upon her, overwhelming her with work
and anxiety.

The Queen has laboured conscientiously to discharge
those duties till her health and strength, already shaken
by the utter and ever-abiding desolation which has taken
the place of her former happiness, have been seriously
impaired.

To call upon her to undergo, in addition, the fatigue of

Victoria by Bertha von Muller
after Joachim von Angeli

those mere State ceremonies which can be equally well performed by other members of her family is to ask her to run the risk of entirely disabling herself for the discharge of those other duties which cannot be neglected without serious injury to the public interests.

The Queen will, however, do what she can – in the manner least trying to her health, strength and spirits – to meet the loyal wishes of her subjects, to afford that support and countenance to society, and to give that encouragement to trade which is desired of her.

Over the years Victoria's grief for her husband did not abate. Her sense of loss remained as acute thirty-nine years after his death as at the time, as she records in her *Journal*:

In this house, that he animated with his humor and rare, wonderful mind, I see him, hear him, search for him everywhere! I go more out of doors; I even take out my pony and ride a little in the beautiful mountains. Then every evening comes the terrible return home, which is so agonizing to me! The house is empty, quiet, desolate! Where is he? I still listen in the hope that he may yet come in, his door may open and his angelic form will return. I could go mad from the desire and longing! Oh, how bitter, how hot are the tears that I often pour forth in the evening in his room, kneeling beside his chair! How fervently do I implore his aid, and how I wring my hands towards heaven and cry aloud: 'Oh, God, have pity, let me go soon! Albert, Albert, come for me.'

This ever dear day has returned again without my beloved Albert being with me, who on this day eighty-one years ago came into the world as a blessing to so many, leaving an imperishable name behind him! How I remember the happy day it used to be, and preparing presents for him which he would like. All, all is engraven on my mind and in my heart. Oh, Albert, it cannot be much longer. If you only knew the loss, the grievous loss you left in my life. No one knows what a load of sorrow and utter loneliness belongs to that saddest of names, a widow. I am afraid that you will no longer be able to say that I am pretty, and I worry at the thought of you seeing me like this. Only remember me as I was, my dearest, and that I love you always. And tell me that you approve of what I have done with the children. I regret the deaths of the three dear ones,

but Bertie and the others are well and strong, and our
thirty-seven great-grandchildren include the crown heads of
Germany and Russia. I thought you'd be proud of that.
There have been so many things I would not do if I had to
do it all over; I only did wearisome things with the
thought that it was good in your eyes. If there were faults,
it was because I did not have your blessed hand to guide me.
But I have tried, with every feeling in my heart, to do what
you would have wished, and I hope you will be pleased.

**Victoria reigned for sixty-four years and became the
epitome of all that was meant by 'Victorian England'.**

The final years were years of apotheosis. In the dazzled
imagination of her subjects Victoria soared aloft towards
the regions of divinity through a nimbus of purest glory.
Criticism fell dumb; deficiencies which, twenty years
earlier, would have been universally admitted, were now
as universally ignored. That the nation's idol was a very
incomplete representative of the nation was a circumstance
that was hardly noticed, and yet it was conspicuously true.
For the vast changes which, out of the England of 1837, had
produced the England of 1897, seemed scarcely to have
touched the Queen.

The evening had been golden; but, after all, the day was
to close in cloud and tempest. Imperial needs, imperial
ambitions, involved the country in the South African War.
There were checks, reverses, bloody disasters; for a moment
the nation was shaken, and the public distresses were felt
with intimate solicitude by the Queen. But her spirit was
high, and neither her courage nor her confidence wavered
for a moment. Throwing herself heart and soul into the
struggle, she laboured with redoubled vigour, interested
herself in every detail of the hostilities, and sought by every
means in her power to render service to the national cause.
In April 1900, when she was in her eighty-first year, she
made the extraordinary decision to abandon her annual
visit to the South of France, and to go instead to Ireland,
which had provided a particularly large number of recruits
to the armies in the field. She stayed for three weeks in
Dublin, driving through the streets, in spite of the warnings
of her advisers, without an armed escort; and the visit was
a complete success. But, in the course of it, she began, for
the first time, to show signs of the fatigue of age. For the

long strain and the unceasing anxiety, brought by the war, made themselves felt at last.

By the end of the year the last remains of her ebbing strength had almost deserted her; and through the early days of the opening century it was clear that her dwindling forces were kept together only by an effort of will. On January 14, she had at Osborne an hour's interview with Lord Roberts, who had returned victorious from South Africa a few days before. She inquired with acute anxiety into all the details of the war; she appeared to sustain the exertion successfully; but, when the audience was over, there was a collapse. On the following day her medical attendants recognised that her state was hopeless; and yet, for two days more, the indomitable spirit fought on; for two days more she discharged the duties of a Queen of England. But after that there was an end of working; and then, and not till then, did the last optimism of those about her break down. The brain was failing, and life was gently slipping away. Her family gathered round her; for a little more she lingered, speechless and apparently insensible; and, on January 22, 1901, she died.

From Lytton Strachey *Queen Victoria*.

Edward VII   1901–1910

'The King arrived at Newmarket shortly before 2 o'clock yesterday, having travelled from London by motor-car. Lunch was served in his majesty's private room at the rustic bungalow fronting the course, and during the afternoon the King spent some time strolling about the plantation walks. There was a cooling breeze blowing across the heath. After the racing concluded the King drove to his rooms at the Jockey Club.'

George V   1910–1936

'Their Majesties honoured with Their presence the Special Performance in aid of King George's Pension Fund for Actors and Actresses, which was given at the Adelphi Theatre, this afternoon.'

Edward VIII   1936

'The King visited the Unemployment Training Centres at Slough and Park Royal this morning.'

George VI   1936–1952

'The King and Queen this evening visited the Spring Show of the Royal Horticultural Society in the Gardens of the Royal Hospital, Chelsea.'

Elizabeth II   1952–

'The Queen this morning visited the Aberdeen Association of Social Service. . . . This afternoon Her Majesty drove to Hazlehead Academy and was received by the Convenor of the Education Committee. The Queen declared the Academy open and unveiled a Commemorative Plaque.'

From the Court Circular of *The Times*, July 1, 1908, June 3, 1924, June 13, 1936, May 26, 1948, and October 7, 1970.

EPILOGUE

And thus they fought all the long day till it was near night, and by that time was there an hundred thousand laid dead upon the down. Then the King looked about him, and then was he ware, of all his host and all his good Knights, were left no more on live but two Knights; that one was Sir Lucan the Butler, and his brother, Sir Bedivere, and they were full sore wounded. 'Jesu mercy,' said the King, 'Where are all my noble Knights become? Alas that ever I should see this doleful day, for now I am come to mine end.'

'Therefore', said Arthur unto Sir Bedivere, 'Take thou Excalibur, my good sword, and go with it to yonder water side; and when thou comest there, I charge thee throw my sword in that water, and come again and tell me what thou there seest.' 'My lord,' said Bedivere, 'your commandment shall be done; and lightly bring you word again.'

So Sir Bedivere departed, and by the way he beheld that noble sword, that the pommel and the haft was all of precious stones, and then he said to himself, 'If I throw this rich sword in the water, thereof shall never come good, but harm and loss.' And then Sir Bedivere hid Excalibur under a tree. And so as soon as he might, he came again unto the King, and said he had been at the water and had thrown the sword into the water. 'What sawest thou there?' said the King; 'Sir,' he said, 'I saw nothing but waves and winds.' 'That is untruly said of thee,' said the King, 'Therefore go though lightly again and do my command, as thou art to me lief and dear; spare not, but throw it in.'

Then Sir Bedivere returned again and took the sword in his hand, and then him thought sin and shame to throw away that noble sword, and so efte [again] he hid the sword, and returned again and told to the King that he had been at the water and done his commandment. 'What saw thou there?' said the King. 'Sir,' he said, 'I saw nothing but the waters wap [beat] and waves wanne [ebb].' 'Ah! traitor untrue,' said King Arthur, 'now thou hast betrayed me twice. Who would have wente [thought] that thou hast been to me so lief and dear, and thou art named a noble knight, and would betray me for the riches of the sword? But now go again lightly, for thy long tarrying putteth me in great jeopardy of my life. For I have taken cold, and but if [except] thou do now as I bid thee, if ever I may see thee I shall slay thee with mine own hands, for thou wouldest for my rich sword see me dead.'

Then Sir Bedivere departed, and went to the sword and lightly took it up, and went to the water side and there he bound the girdle about the hilts, and then he threw the sword as far into the water as he might, and there came an arm and an hand above the water and met it, and caught it and so shook it thrice and brandished, and then vanished away the hand with the sword in the water. So Sir Bedivere came again to the King and told him what he saw. 'Alas!' said the King, 'help me hence for I dread me I have tarried over long.'

Then Sir Bedivere took the King upon his back and so went with him to that water side, and when they were at the water side, even fast by the bank hoved [floated] a little barge with many fair ladies in it, and among them all was a queen, and they all had black hoods, and they all wept and shrieked when they saw King Arthur.

'Now put me into the barge,' said the King, and so he did softly. And there received him three queens with great mourning, and so they set him down, and in one of their laps King Arthur laid his head, and then that queen said, 'Ah, dear brother, why have ye tarried so long from me? Alas, this wound on your head hath caught overmuch cold.' And so then they rowed from the land, and Sir Bedivere beheld all those ladies go from him. Then Sir Bedivere cried, 'Ah, my lord Arthur, what shall become of me now ye go from me, and leave me here alone among mine enemies?' 'Comfort thyself,' said the King 'and do as well as thou mayst; for in me is no trust for to trust in. For I will into the vale of Avilion, to heal me of my grievous wound. And if thou hear never more of me, pray for my soul.' But ever the queens and ladies wept and shrieked, that was pity to hear. And as soon Sir Bedivere had lost sight of the barge, he wept and wailed, and so took to the forest, and he went all that night.

Thus of Arthur I find never more written in books that can be authorised, nor more of the certainty of his death heard I never tell but that he was led away.

Yet some men yet say in many parts of England that King Arthur is not dead, but had by the will of our Lord Jesu in another place. And men say that he shall come again, and he shall win the holy cross. I will not say that it shall be so, but rather will I say, here in this world he changed his life. But many men say that there is written upon his tomb: 'Hic jacet Arthurus rex, quondam rex que futurus'
THE ONCE AND FUTURE KING.

From Sir Thomas Malory *The Morte d'Arthur*.

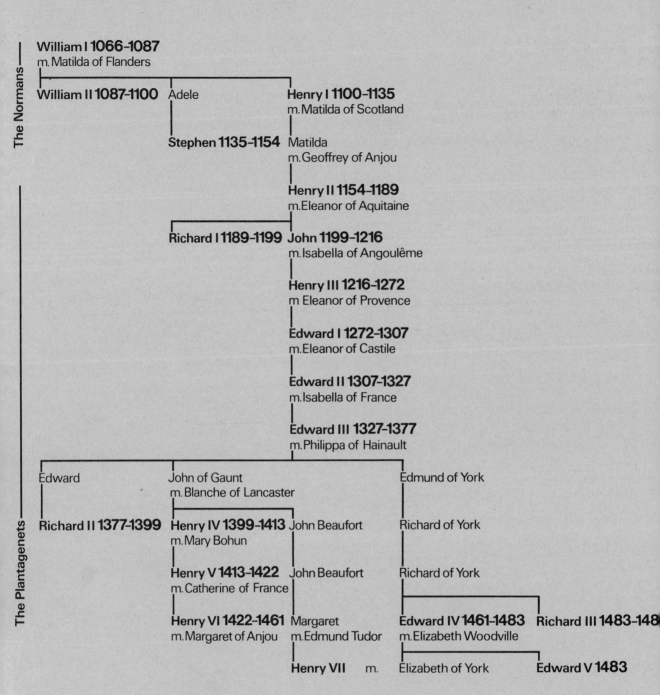

The Normans

William I 1066–1087
m. Matilda of Flanders

William II 1087–1100   Adele   **Henry I 1100–1135**
m. Matilda of Scotland

Stephen 1135–1154   Matilda
m. Geoffrey of Anjou

Henry II 1154–1189
m. Eleanor of Aquitaine

Richard I 1189–1199   **John 1199–1216**
m. Isabella of Angoulême

Henry III 1216–1272
m Eleanor of Provence

Edward I 1272–1307
m. Eleanor of Castile

Edward II 1307–1327
m. Isabella of France

Edward III 1327–1377
m. Philippa of Hainault

The Plantagenets

Edward   John of Gaunt   Edmund of York
m. Blanche of Lancaster

Richard II 1377–1399   **Henry IV 1399–1413**   John Beaufort   Richard of York
m. Mary Bohun

Henry V 1413–1422   John Beaufort   Richard of York
m. Catherine of France

Henry VI 1422–1461   Margaret   **Edward IV 1461–1483**   **Richard III 1483–148**
m. Margaret of Anjou   m. Edmund Tudor   m. Elizabeth Woodville

Henry VII   m.   Elizabeth of York   **Edward V 1483**